P.16 Quant/Qual differences

P.21 - don't feed back

- expensive: first qual int, easier to use proper methods then last

To Julie
Best regards,
Grant

THE LONG INTERVIEW

GRANT McCRACKEN
University of Guelph,
Guelph, Ontario, Canada

Qualitative Research Methods,
Volume 13

SAGE PUBLICATIONS
The Publishers of Professional Social Science
Newbury Park   Beverly Hills   London   New Delhi

For information address:

SAGE Publications, Inc.
2111 West Hillcrest Drive
Newbury Park, California 91320

SAGE Publications Inc.
275 South Beverly Drive
Beverly Hills
California 90212

SAGE Publications Ltd.
28 Banner Street
London EC1Y 8QE
England

SAGE PUBLICATIONS India Pvt. Ltd.
M-32 Market
Greater Kailash I
New Delhi 110 048 India

Printed in the United States of America

Library of Congress Cataloging-in-Publication Data

McCracken, Grant David, 1951-
    The long interview / Grant McCracken.
        p.   cm. — (Qualitative research methods ; v. 13)
    Bibliography: p.
    ISBN 0-8039-3352-5   ISBN 0-8039-3353-3 (pbk.)
    1. Social sciences—Research—Methodology.   2. Interviewing.
I. Title.   II. Series.
H61.M4815   1988
300'.723—dc19   88-14017
                                                       CIP

FIRST PRINTING 1988

When citing a University Paper, please use the proper form. Remember to cite the correct Sage University Paper series title and include the paper number. One of the following formats can be adapted (depending on the style manual used):

(1) KIRK, JEROME and MARC L. MILLER (1986) Reliability and Validity in Qualitative Research. Sage University Paper Series on Qualitative Research Methods, Vol. 1. Beverly Hills, CA: Sage.

or

(2) Kirk, J., & Miller, M. L. (1986). *Reliability and validity in qualitative research* (Sage University Paper Series on Qualitative Research Methods, Vol. 1). Beverly Hills, CA: Sage.

CONTENTS

EDITORS' INTRODUCTION

Grant McCracken presents in Volume 13 of the Qualitative Research Methods Series a modern blueprint for research attuned to pragmatic constraints. McCracken promotes the long interview as the method of choice when cultural categories, assumptions, and themes are objects of investigation, and when total immersion in the studied scene is impractical or impossible. Showing that interviewing competence can be taught, McCracken demystifies the role of the qualitative researcher. In a thorough and student-friendly way, he instructs us about the strengths, limits, and subtleties of the method. Topics examined in detail concern the review of literature and the researcher's own understandings of culture, the design of open-ended questionnaires, the interview experience, the analysis of data, and the packaging of findings. In all of this, Professor McCracken is careful not to overstate his case, promoting an interview plan that meshes well with a number of qualitative and nonqualitative techniques. The value and mechanics of the long ethnographic interview have deserved attention for some time. This volume nicely accomplishes the task.

—Marc L. Miller
John Van Maanen
Peter K. Manning

PREFACE AND ACKNOWLEDGMENTS

This book gives a systematic guide to the theory and method of the long qualitative interview. Its object is to introduce the reader to (1) key theoretical and methodological issues, (2) vigorous research strategies, and (3) a simple four-step model of inquiry. It is designed to give social scientists and their students a clear, comprehensive, and practical model of one of the most powerful techniques in the qualitative methodology.

The long interview has a special place in the qualitative methodology. We may distinguish it from the unstructured "ethnographic" interview, participant observation, the focus group, and the depth interview.

It departs from the unstructured "ethnographic" interview insofar as it adopts a deliberately more efficient and less obtrusive format. It is a sharply focused, rapid, highly intensive interview process that seeks to diminish the indeterminacy and redundancy that attends more unstructured research processes. The long interview calls for special kinds of preparation and structure, including the use of an open-ended questionnaire, so that the investigator can maximize the value of the time spent with the respondent. It also calls for special patterns of analysis so that the investigator can maximize the value of the time spent analyzing the data. In other words, the long interview is designed to give the investigator a highly efficient, productive, "stream-lined" instrument of inquiry.

The long interview departs from participant observation insofar as it is intended to accomplish certain ethnographic objectives without committing the investigator to intimate, repeated, and prolonged involvement in the life and community of the respondent. It departs from group methods of qualitative research (such as the focus group) insofar as it is conducted between the investigator and a single respondent. It departs from the "depth" interview practiced by the psychological inquirer in so far as it is concerned with cultural categories and shared meanings rather than individual affective states. These characteristics give the long interview special strengths and advantages that this book hopes to put at the reader's disposal.

The book opens with a general overview of the character and purpose of qualitative inquiry. The second chapter reviews the key issues that confront qualitative methods in general and the long interview in particular. The third chapter outlines each of the four steps of the long qualitative interview. The fourth chapter suggests one way to maintain and judge the quality of this qualitative work. The fifth chapter talks about strategies for writing up the results of qualitative research; this chapter is intended especially for students who have relatively little experience in this difficult area. The sixth chapter considers the management of qualitative research, and offers practical advice for those who commission and administer this research. The last chapter offers a brief conclusion. The book ends with four appendices, which are designed to simplify research design, preparation, and training. They include a sample questionnaire for biographical data, a standard ethics protocol, a list of budget considerations, and a number of topics appropriate for training in qualitative methods.

As an anthropologist in an interdisciplinary college, I am frequently asked to give advice on qualitative methods. My colleagues represent diverse fields: gerontology, public policy, nutrition, sociology, social psychology, design, environmental psychology, consumer behavior, product development, and management. All are keen to add qualitative methods to their research armories. When these colleagues ask me for reading suggestions, I am unable to recommend anything with enthusiasm. No single text seems to me to capture the power of the long interview and transcend its equally considerable difficulties. I wrote the present book to create such a text. I hope it will prove useful.

Many debts have been incurred in the writing of this book. Thanks are due to Victor Roth, John Van Maanen, and Linda Wood for their very useful comments on the manuscript, and to Elizabeth Upton, Alex Michalos, Zak Sabrey, Russ Belk, and Laurie Sims for key pieces of advice. Thanks are also due to students who have taken my Qualitative Research Methods course. My deepest debt is to my teachers (especially Marshall Sahlins and David Schneider) at the University of Chicago, where my formal training in qualitative methods began, and to Mish Vadasz, from whom I was lucky enough to get my early training.

THE LONG INTERVIEW

GRANT McCRACKEN
University of Guelph

1. INTRODUCTION

The long interview is one of the most powerful methods in the qualitative armory. For certain descriptive and analytic purposes, no instrument of inquiry is more revealing. The method can take us into the mental world of the individual, to glimpse the categories and logic by which he or she sees the world. It can also take us into the lifeworld of the individual, to see the content and pattern of daily experience. The long interview gives us the opportunity to step into the mind of another person, to see and experience the world as they do themselves.

The applications of such an instrument are, of course, endless. Every social scientific study is improved by a clearer understanding of the beliefs and experience of the actors in question. For instance, the quantitative study concerned with birth rates is improved by the knowledge of how social actors define and experience "family," "parenthood," "child rearing," and so on. The study devoted to economic expenditure is improved by an understanding of the cultural matters that inform the acts of getting and spending. Without these understandings, our vision of social scientific data is monocular when it could be binocular. Without a qualitative understanding of how culture mediates human action, we can know only what the numbers tell us. The long qualitative interview is useful because it can help us to situate these numbers in their fuller social and cultural context.

9

In other cases, qualitative methods and the long interview are compelling, almost obligatory. It is difficult to imagine a study of "friendship," for instance, that does not inquire into how people define a friend, how they experience a friendship, and the silent assumptions that operate in every social situation to dictate how friends and nonfriends act. The long interview lets us map out the organizing ideas of friendship and determine how these ideas enter into the individual's view of the world. It also lets us see how friendship works as a constituent of the individual's daily experience.

But there is a third class of research that invites qualitative research: the applied social sciences. As my colleagues demonstrate daily, social scientists now apply their skills to a wide range of urgent issues. They seek to determine the best relocation strategies for the elderly, how day care can be adapted to the needs of the single parent, how to establish new product development strategies, what the two-parent, single-child family wants in the design of a condominium, to give just a few local examples. These are issues that cry out for qualitative treatment. What does "home" mean to the elderly, how does a single mother organize her time, what is "innovation" for management, and what bundle of attitudes, interests, and activities is the urban nuclear family? The application of the social sciences to the study and improvement of contemporary life depends upon these intimate understandings of the respondent.

But if qualitative methods are important, their use in the study of modern societies is not by any means straightforward. The difficulty is that respondents lead hectic, deeply segmented, and privacy-centered lives. Even the most willing of them have only limited time and attention to give the investigator. Qualitative methods may have the power to take the investigator into the minds and lives of the respondents, to capture them warts and all. But few respondents are willing to sit for all the hours it takes to complete the portrait.

Some social scientists are unconcerned with this shortage of time. In the conventional field setting, the anthropologist can insinuate him- or herself into the life of the community gradually and by stages. He or she can take many months of inquiry and exposure to construct an understanding of the community's world view and daily life. Plainly, however, the rigors and demands of this kind of qualitative inquiry are extremely high. Few social scientists have this much time at their disposal. Indeed, most are no richer in time than their respondents. Rarely can they suspend the demands of teaching, administration, other research projects, and their own private lives sufficiently to create the vast blocks of time that participant observation demands.

But it is also true that certain vital arenas of modern life are simply closed to social scientific scrutiny. For instance, no North American family is likely to suffer the presence of an observer for an extended period of time. Public and private corporations are equally unenthusiastic about an observer who has no stake in the proceedings. Political parties have similar scruples, as do a range of special interest groups. North Americans value, depend upon, and vigorously defend their privacy. They are loath to see it breached. As a result, social scientists are denied the opportunity of participating as observers in the lives of many of the people they wish to understand.

These two factors, time scarcity and concern for privacy, stand as important impediments to the qualitative study of modern life. It is precisely these impediments that make the long interview so valuable as a means of inquiry. For this research strategy gives us access to individuals without violating their privacy or testing their patience. It allows us to capture the data needed for penetrating qualitative analysis without participant observation, unobtrusive observation, or prolonged contact. It allows us, in other words, to achieve crucial qualitative objectives within a manageable methodological context.

2. NINE KEY ISSUES

There are several areas of controversy within qualitative research methodology. One of these concerns the way in which the qualitative research community has fashioned, or refused to fashion, a relationship to the several social sciences and alternative methods of social scientific study. As we shall see, this point has proven explosively controversial. Some qualitative researchers have chosen to look beyond their own borders to other methods and many disciplines. Others have insisted on the virtue of tending their own garden. The methodology presented here comes down very firmly on the side of the former.

The second compelling question concerns the relationship between the researcher and his or her own culture. This issue takes us to the very heart of the great potential and the great difficulty of qualitative methodology. It is precisely because the qualitative researchers are working in their own culture that they can make the long interview do such powerful work. It is by drawing on their understanding of how they themselves see and experience the world that they can supplement and interpret the data they generate in the long interview. Just as plainly, however, this intimate acquaintance with one's own culture can create as much blindness as insight. It can prevent the observer from seeing cultural assumptions and practices. The long interview presented here is deliberately designed to take advantage of the opportunity for insight and minimize the dangers of familiarity.

The third concerns the relationship between the researcher and the data. The key question here is: How can the researcher collect data that are both abundant and manageable? As we shall observe below, every qualitative interview is, potentially, a Pandora's box generating endlessly various and abundant data. The problem is to control the kind and amount of these data without also artificially constraining or forcing their character. This long interview is designed to take account of this problem as well.

The fourth concerns the relationship between the researcher and the respondent. How is this delicate relationship best constructed and construed? The long interview is a highly unusual speech event, one that makes for a most peculiar social relationship. There is no question that certain aspects of this event and relationship must be very exactly crafted (and manipulated) to serve the interests of good qualitative inquiry. But we must also take care to observe the rights (formal and informal) of the respondent. The method presented here seeks to take advantage of the qualitative opportunity without also taking advantage of the respondent.

These are four problem areas that any methodology in the qualitative literature must contend with. We shall see that these problems areas diverge and intersect to form several different configurations. In order to deal with them individually and in concert, I have treated them below in the form of nine key issues.

Issue 1:   The Social Scientific Research Community

What kind of relationship should exist between qualitative research and other methods of social scientific inquiry? There is no consensus here. Some qualitative researchers look for cooperation. Others have chosen a different posture. There are qualitative researchers who insist that they cannot fully belong to the social scientific world because they have been forced to live for so long at its margins. Some claim that they do not wish to belong because their qualitative methods give them privileged access to proprietary truths. Still others argue that they are already the secret elite of this world for it is only they who can grasp and use the magical methods of the qualitative tradition. Qualitative researchers have mustered several, quite flattering, arguments with which to distance themselves from the other social sciences.

The evidence for these "special status" arguments is largely arti-factual. It is largely because there are few clear operational standards for training in, and the practice of, qualitative methods, that these methods are now used chiefly by a small group of scholars blessed with "special" abilities. Without these standards, qualitative researchers could not but remain a marginal presence in the social sciences. Without these standards, qualitative truths appeared somehow more evanescent than quantitative ones. Without these standards, qualitative methods were, necessarily, only within the reach of the "naturally" gifted.

It is, in other words, largely the failings of the field, not the special status of its practitioners, that have encouraged both "ghetto" protests and "magic circle" pretensions. Let us demonstrate that qualitative methods can be routinized and made accessible to all. As Merton, Fiske, and Kendall (1956: 17) insisted, some 30 years ago, qualitative interviewing is no "private and incommunicable art."

It is time for the field of qualitative methods to make itself a full citizen of the social sciences. If the field fails to move from defensive postures to constructive ones, and if it fails to begin to systematize and routinize qualitative methods, it can expect to lose the constituency in the social scientific community that now looks to it with interest. It is time to stop proclaiming, and to start demonstrating, the value of qualitative methods. This is a critical moment in the development of qualitative methods because, in the forceful but apposite language of everyday speech, it is time for qualitative partisans to "put up or shut up."

Issue 2:   The Donor Social Sciences—
A Call for Ecumenical Cooperation

But taking up full citizenship in the social sciences is only the first of the qualitative researcher's new responsibilities. It is also necessary to bring the several "tribes" of the qualitative tradition into a state of useful cooperation. The goal of cooperation is complicated by the great diversity of approach that exists here. The development of each of these subgroups in the qualitative community has been fitful, divergent, and uncoordinated.

Sociology witnessed an explosion of activity in the 1950s.[1] Directed or inspired by the Chicago School (Thomas, 1983), researchers took these new methods into medical schools (Becker, 1956), Pentecostal churches (Von Hoffman and Cassidy, 1956), forbidden communities (Lezner, 1956), the homes of the upper classes (Seeley et al., 1956), and every nook and cranny of entire communities (Warner and Lunt, 1941). Much of this work was designed to aid in the practice of participant observation. But because it is also designed for the study of North American societies, we shall find it useful in this study of the long interview proposed here.

The winter of positivism that prevailed in the social sciences in the 1960s and 1970s cut short much of sociology's enthusiasm for qualitative methods. Indeed, these methods might have passed altogether from the field were it not for the vigorous and brilliant efforts of Glaser and Strauss (1965, 1968) and Schatzman and Strauss (1973). This work also presumes a participant observation mode, but is useful for the creation of a model of the long qualitative interview. One of the special virtues of this work, and one of the things that accounts for its wide spread influence in the social sciences, is the scheme it proposes for data analysis. This will be referred to below.

Happily, there is now a qualitative revival underway in sociology. This new generation of scholarship continues to concentrate on participant observation, but it now draws on several disparate traditions, including symbolic interactionism, phenomenology, hermenuetics, ethnomethodology, interpretive sociology, and antipositivists of all kinds.[2]

Psychology, another victim of the winter of positivism, has cultivated qualitative methods more routinely for clinical purposes than research ones (e.g., LaRossa and Wolf, 1985; Sullivan, 1954). Happily, this field is also beginning to show new interest in qualitative methods, and diverse theoretical orientations are at work here as well, including ethogenics, narrative psychology, and phenomenology.[3]

Anthropology, never the captive of positivist enthusiasms, helped to keep the qualitative faith alive in the 1950s and 1960s. However, for all of its practical commitment, it failed to formalize or articulate its methods. As a result, the field perhaps best situated to contribute to the methodological literature has contributed relatively little (Stocking, 1983: 112). With a few notable exceptions (e.g., DuBois, 1937;

Kluckhohn, 1940; Paul, 1953), the field has, until recently, created a surprisingly thin methodological literature and virtually no pedagogical tradition (Nash and Wintrob, 1972). It is worth pointing out, for instance, that students passed through the master's and Ph.D. programs in anthropology at a major American research university in the mid-1970s without taking so much as a single course in methodology. In the absence of this training, the field has relied on its own oral tradition to pass methods from one generation of scholars to the next. Just as often, each generation has had to reinvent these methods for itself. Happily, this methodological somnolence appears finally at an end.[4]

Evaluation research and administrative sciences also understood the value of qualitative methods at a time when other social sciences had forsaken them. These fields were, however, perhaps more reflexive and systematic than their anthropological brethren, and developed a rich theoretical and practical body of literature.[5]

Caught up in the preoccupations of positivism, consumer research has been unprepared, until recently, to credit any but the most limited range of qualitative methods as useful. Even here, in the development of the focus group, there has been substantially more concern with practice than theory.[6] Recently, a broader range of qualitative methods has been developed and applied.[7]

The "fits and starts" development, and heterogeneous character, of the qualitative community has discouraged the creation of robust research agenda and well-worked theoretical models. Moreover, it has allowed each subgroup to neglect the work being done in other fields. The key issue here, then, is that future research must be coordinated and ecumenical. It is now longer enough to pursue research on an ad hoc basis, and it is no longer possible to ignore the research activities and accomplishments of other fields. Too little work has been done on this question for any of us to afford the luxury of disciplinary isolationism.

As this coordinated undertaking develops, it is worth wondering whether any particular social science will emerge as the central "donor discipline" for qualitative methods (as statistics now is for quantitative ones). It is possible that sociolinguistics will claim this position. It can already provide a very precise understanding of some of the mechanics of the qualitative interview (Briggs, 1986; Churchill, 1973), and none of the social sciences is better placed to judge the delicate and subtle interactive processes of which the interview consists.[8] For these microcosmic issues, in any case, sociolinguistics has much to contribute.

There are many other fields that may someday exert an influence here. There is not yet an "anthropology of the interview" in anthropology, but this cannot be far off. There is also reason to think that someday we will see systematic studies of the interview that examine it from the point of view of semiotics, symbolic interactionism, and phenomenology.

Issue 3: The Qualitative/Quantitative Difference

This issue has been well argued in several places.[9] I wish merely to develop what I take to be the most telling and important differences between the qualitative and quantitative traditions.

Perhaps the most striking difference between the methods is the way in which each tradition treats its analytic categories. The quantitative goal is to isolate and define categories as precisely as possible before the study is undertaken, and then to determine, again with great precision, the relationship between them. The qualitative goal, on the other hand, is often to isolate and define categories during the process of research. The qualitative investigator expects the nature and definition of analytic categories to change in the course of a project (Glaser and Strauss, 1965). For one field, well defined categories are the means of research, for another they are the object of research.

Still more strikingly, the qualitative research normally looks for patterns of interrelationship between many categories rather than the sharply delineated relationship between a limited set of them. This difference can be characterized as the trade-off between the precision of quantitative methods and the complexity-capturing ability of qualitative ones. The quantitative researcher uses a lens that brings a narrow strip of the field of vision into very precise focus. The qualitative researcher uses a lens that permits a much less precise vision of a much broader strip.

Another of the differences between these methods turns on the data-reporting abilities of the respondent. Some social scientific questions elicit easy and rapid responses from the respondent. The respondent can identify precisely what is wanted, retrieve it easily, and report it without ambiguity. Other questions are much more demanding. The respondent has more difficulty determining what is wanted. He or she must then labor to identify and articulate a response. This difference between reporting abilities is, effectively, one of the differences between qualitative and quantitative methods. When the questions for which data are sought allows the respondent to respond readily and unambiguously, closed questions and quantitative methods are indicated. When the questions for which data are sought are likely to cause the respondent greater difficulty and imprecision, the broader, more flexible net provided by qualitative techniques is appropriate.

A final difference between qualitative and quantitative approaches is the number and kind of respondents that should be recruited for research purposes. The quantitative project requires investigators to construct a "sample" of the necessary size and type to generalize to the larger population. In the qualitative case, however, the issue is not one of generalizability. It is that of access. The purpose of the qualitative interview is not to discover how many, and what kinds of, people share a certain characteristic. It is to gain access to the cultural categories and assumptions according to which one culture construes the world. How many and what kinds of people hold these categories and assumptions is not, in fact, the compelling issue. It is the categories and assumptions, not those who hold them, that matter. In other words, qualitative research does not survey the terrain, it mines it. It is, in other words, much more intensive than extensive in its objectives.

The selection of respondents must be made accordingly. The first principle is that "less is more." It is more important to work longer, and with greater care, with a few people than more superficially with many of them. For many research projects, eight respondents will be perfectly sufficient. The quantitatively trained social scientist reels at the thought of so small a "sample," but it is important to remember that this group is not chosen to represent some part of the larger world. It offers, instead, an opportunity to glimpse the complicated character, organization, and logic of culture. How widely what is discovered exists in the rest of the world cannot be decided by qualitative methods, but only by quantitative ones. It is, precisely, this "division of labor" that makes the cooperative use of qualitative and quantitative methods so important to the qualitative investigator. It is only after the qualitative investigator has taken advantage of quantitative research that he or she is prepared to determine the distribution and frequency of the culture phenomenon that has come to light.

These differences between qualitative and quantitative methods have several implications. The first is that the two research approaches represent two very different sets of intellectual habits and frames of mind. This must be kept in mind when one tradition seeks to master, or to judge, the other. For instance, even after qualitative methods have been made more transparent and routine, students from the quantitative tradition will not be able to master qualitative methods merely by learning a few techniques (any more than the qualitative practitioner can pretend to have mastered quantitative methods through the mastery of, say, regression analysis). Learning the qualitative tradition will require the absorption of new assumptions and "ways of seeing." It will require new strategies of conceptualizing research problems and data.

Second, the qualitative and quantitative approaches are never substitutes for one another. This is so because, necessarily, they observe different realities, or different aspects of the same reality. This distinctness must be honored. One cannot draw quantitative conclusions from qualitative work. Overholser (1986) notes the tendency of some qualitative researchers to speak of their results in quantitative terms. These investigators observe that "all," "some," "slightly more than half" of their respondents expressed a certain opinion, as if this were a useful or legitimate way to talk about the data. Falciglia, Wahlbrink, and Suszkiw (1985) evidence this tendency when, after more than 1,500 hours of observation with the sample of four respondents, they offer conclusions of a strongly quantitative character. Quantitative standards have been so deeply embedded in the "culture" of the social sciences that it may be some time before we are free of the tendency to judge qualitative methods by quantitative standards.

But it is also true that quantitative research never obviates the need for qualitative research. The literature is full of examples of individuals who have used their quantitative data to tell us how people think about and experience the world. In sum, a keen regard for what each of these methods can, and cannot, do is essential. Only thus can we learn to use them in conjunction and exploit their respective analytic advantages.

Issue 4: Investigator as Instrument

In qualitative research, the investigator serves as a kind of "instrument" in the collection and analysis of data (Cassell, 1977: 414; Guba and Lincoln, 1981: 128-152; Reeves Sanday, 1979: 528; Schwartz and Schwartz, 1955: 343). This metaphor is a useful one because it emphasizes that the investigator cannot fulfill qualitative research objectives without using a broad range of his or her own experience, imagination, and intellect in ways that are various and unpredictable (Miles, 1979: 597).

It is especially the complexity and depth of the qualitative research enterprise that encourages this aspect of qualitative methods. Qualitative data are normally relatively messy, unorganized data. It demands techniques of observation that allow the investigator to sort and "winnow" the data, searching out patterns of association and assumption. This process of detection is hard to mechanize. It is necessary to listen not only with the tidiest and most precise of one's cognitive abilities, but also with the whole of one's experience and imagination. Detection proceeds by a kind of "rummaging" process. The investigator must use his or her experience and imagination to find (or fashion) a match for the patterns evidenced by the data. The diverse aspects of the self become a bundle of templates to be held up against the data until parallels emerge.

It is this "self as instrument" aspect of qualitative inquiry that has inspired some of the spurious claims referred to above. Some qualitative practitioners have used the "whole person" concept to argue that qualitative methods are best used by enchanted, artistic souls in the revelation of veiled and sacred truths. But let us say this plainly: The "self as instrument" notion is no warrant for romantic visions of qualitative research. The fundamentals of these methods are straightforward and transmittable. Even mortals can master and practice them. Someday we shall see these methods pass routinely between even the most disenchanted teacher and unenchanting student.

The self-as-instrument process works most easily when it is used simply to search out a match in one's experience for ideas and actions that the respondent has described in the interview. In my own research, I thought through the implications of one respondent's comments on his relationship with his grandchildren by rummaging through what I know about my own family relationships, the relationship I recall having with my grandfathers, and the relationship I have with nephews and nieces. This matching activity helped me see that this grandfather felt an interesting combination of delight and anxiety for a relationship in which he had no parental responsibility (the delight) but over which he had no parental control (the anxiety). The matching process helped fill in and flesh out what the respondent meant to say.

It is worth emphasizing that there is no simple one-to-one relationship in this matching process. There is no crude transfer from the investigator's experience to that of the respondent. On the contrary, the investigator's experience is merely a bundle of possibilities, pointers, and suggestions that can be used to plumb the remarks of a respondent.

Even quite plausible matches require substantiation and confirmation from the remainder of the interview analysis. They must be confirmed over and over before they are admissible as evidence.

Sometimes, there is no match to be found in the investigator's own experience. In these cases the investigator must proceed by fashioning an understanding of what is being said. The process of imaginative reconstruction is somewhat more difficult than the matching technique. It requires the investigator to build an alien, mysterious world of meaning out of assertions that are themselves unconnected, new, or strange. They must perform this task using their own categories of everyday thought, categories that neither anticipate nor welcome the new configuration of meaning. This is an essentially difficult undertaking. The investigator is like an inhabitant of the rain forest trying to imagine an adobe hut.

The process of imaginative reconstruction can be undertaken in several ways. One of the most effective of these requires the investigator to treat the respondent's new and strange propositions as if they were simply and utterly true. The investigator must let these ideas live in his or her own mind as if they were the most natural of assumptions. Once these ideas have been properly "entertained," the investigator can ask: "What does the world look like when I hold these things to be true." When this process succeeds, the investigator has succeeded in reconstructing a version of the respondent's view of the world by taking up and trying on his or her underlying assumptions and categories. If this method is more difficult than matching, it is also potentially more exciting. Its results are often the real achievements of the qualitative methodology.

My own most striking example of this technique came in the middle of an interview I conducted with a 75-year-old woman in the living room of her home (McCracken, 1988a). As we talked about the furnishings of this room, I found myself unable fully to understand her comments unless I gave up some of my own assumptions about the "thingness" of living room furniture. The simple act of following her commentary required me to begin to cast about for another way of seeing. As I listened to her, a new perspective arrived suddenly and with force. "My god," I thought, "this isn't a household, it's a museum. Its furnishings are not inanimate objects and consumer goods, but memorials." Entertaining the respondent's assertions as unexceptional truths is the most demanding but also the most rewarding of the objectives of the self-as-instrument technique.

Issue 5:   The Obtrusive/Unobtrusive Balance

Qualitative methods are most useful and powerful when they are used to discover how the respondent sees the world. This objective of the method makes it essential that testimony be elicited in as unobtrusive, nondirective manner as possible (Brenner, 1985). At crucial moments in the interview, the entire success of the enterprise depends upon drawing out the respondent in precisely the right manner. An error here can prevent the capture of the categories and the logic used by the respondent. It can mean that the project ends up "capturing" nothing more than the investigator's own logic and categories, so that the reminder of the project takes on a dangerously tautological quality.

One of the implications of this principle is that the investigator must not engage what is commonly called "active listening." This strategy encourages the investigator to "read" the hidden meaning of speech and gesture and "play it back" to the respondent. It encourages phrases like "what I hear you saying is . . . ," and "I hear anger in your tone of voice." Active listening strategies must not be used by the qualitative researcher. They are obtrusive in precisely the manner that this research wishes to avoid, and they are likely to be almost completely destructive of good data, as the following excerpt from a qualitative interview transcript illustrates.

> Interviewer: "What did you miss most about being away from your family?"
>
> Respondent: "The family."
>
> Interviewer: "The love and warmth?"

Here, the interviewer violates the law of nondirection, and suggests the terms in which the respondent ought to describe his experience. Happily, the respondent rejects the suggested terms, and proposes his own account.

> Respondent: "The togetherness and that sort of thing, and being able to talk to your family, talk more intimately. In the army the talk is more or less on a lower level."

This is useful and interesting because it sets up a contrast (i.e., between the family and the army) and introduces a hierarchical metaphor (i.e., higher and lower levels of talk). Something of the respondent's view of the world is beginning to emerge and the interviewer need only encourage this unobtrusively. Instead, the interview chooses, once more, to supply terms.

Interviewer: "Surface level?"

This strategy destroys the contrast and the metaphor, and our respondent, who knows bad qualitative research when he sees it, throws in the towel.

Respondent: "Surface level . . . I guess you could call it that."

There is cause, then, for scrupulous attention to this matter. It is important that the investigator allow the respondent to tell his or her own story in his or her own terms. However, it is just as important that the interviewer exercise some control over the interview. Qualitative data are almost always extraordinarily abundant. Every qualitative interview is, potentially, a Pandora's box. Every qualitative researcher is, potentially, the hapless victim of a shapeless inquiry. The scholar who does not control these data will surely sink without a trace.

The question, then, is not whether, but how, to impose order and structure on these data. One of the ways of doing so in the data-collection stage of research is through the construction of a series of "prompts." These are designed to help give structure to the interview. A second way of imposing order is through the construction of a well-designed questionnaire. Both of these will be discussed below in the next chapter.

Issue 6: Manufacturing Distance

Scholars working in another culture have a very great advantage over those who work in their own. Virtually everything before them is, to some degree, mysterious. Those who work in their own culture do not have this critical distance from what they study. They carry with them a large number of assumptions that can create a treacherous sense of familiarity (Chock, 1986: 93; Greenhouse, 1985: 261). With these assumptions in place, an invisible hand directs inquiry and forecloses the range and the kind of things the investigator can observe and understand. As Von Hoffman and Cassidy (1956) put it, "Time and time again we would encounter a symbol, an act, a practice, assume it had a meaning familiar to us, and find later on it did not" (p. 197). In order to avoid this problem it is incumbent on the investigator to "manufacture distance." It is necessary to create a critical awareness of matters with which we have a deep and blinding familiarity (Marcus and Fischer, 1986: 137-164).

But it is not only the investigator who needs to manufacture distance. Most respondents have difficulty giving a full account of what they believe and what they do. Long ago, their beliefs became assumptions and their actions became habits. Both are now almost completely submerged beneath the surface of consciousness. The investigator must help the respondent to recover his or her beliefs and actions from this taken-for-granted state. Here, too, the secret is to manufacture distance.

Investigators can manufacture distance in several ways. They can bring themselves to see with new detachment the categories and assumptions that organize their worlds. The classic method of doing so is to go off to another culture for an extended period of time and then return to one's own. Anthropologists who do this report that they return to a once familiar world with a profound sense of its peculiar and arbitrary character. Plainly, this is not a practical alternative for most social scientists, and other techniques are necessary.

It is worth observing here that there are many informal opportunities for distance manufacture. The events and occurrences of everyday life supply some of these. A good example is the sensation of surprise. Surprise is occasioned by violated expectation, and violated expectation points to the presence of otherwise hidden cultural categories and assumptions. Surprise is, to this extent, an opportunity for distance. Humor is another. Humor very deliberately mixes categories and violates assumptions. Watching how it operates on our expectations can be a useful way of creating distance. Virtually all of the creative arts engage in some form of distance manufacture. As one of its themes, Shakespeare's *King Lear,* for example, takes up what fathers and daughters owe to one another. By observing the structural details of this tragedy, we can stand back from familiar assumptions about familial relations and see them more clearly. In short, our day-to-day experience is rich in observational opportunities. A sharp eye will find manufactured distance at every turn.

One or two social scientists have quite deliberately used distance manufacture as the basis of their observation and analysis. Erving Goffman, in perhaps the most famous case in point, resolved to learn about the rules of social discourse by putting himself in a situation in which he knew they would be violated, a mental institution. As each successive rule of social discourse was broken, Goffman began to see an entire set of principles that invisibly govern everyday life. With every violation of his expectations, distance was manufactured and the subtle rules of social life became clearer.

While investigators are free to experiment variously with their expectations, and see whether they can pry back their sense of familiarity and peer at the world behind, respondents are, understandably, somewhat less enthusiastic about this practice and quite slow to volunteer it on their own. For this group to stand back from categories and assumptions, gentle intervention is required. As we shall see below, one of the ways of creating distance is to establish certain prompting procedures that invite the respondent to articulate what he or she otherwise takes for granted. These prompts can be conversation cues. They can be well-designed questions. They can also be a series of stimuli (such as photographs) in which the respondent is asked to point out and account for similarities and differences amongst the stimuli. Good research helps respondents report their experience by manufacturing the distance they need to do so.

In sum, both the investigator and the respondent need the opportunity to see familiar data in unfamiliar ways. The four-step method proposed in the next chapter discusses how both parties can manufacture distance.

Issue 7: The Questionnaire

The use of a questionnaire is sometimes regarded as a discretionary matter in qualitative research interview. But, for the purposes of the long qualitative interview, it is indispensable. The demanding objectives of this interview require its use (Brenner, 1985).

The questionnaire has several functions. Its first responsibility is to ensure that the investigator covers all the terrain in the same order for each respondent (preserving in a rough way the conversational context of each interview). The second function is the care and scheduling of the prompts necessary to manufacture distance. As we shall see below, these prompts must be carefully crafted, and precisely situated, in the interview. It is too much to expect the interviewer to formulate, or recall, them in the demanding circumstances of the interview. The third function of the questionnaire is that it establishes channels for the direction and scope of discourse. The really open-ended interview is an ever-expanding realm of possibility in which the generative power of language is unleashed to potentially chaotic effect. The fourth function of the questionnaire is that it allows the investigator to give all his or her attention to the informant's testimony. The first responsibility of the interviewer is the highly contingent work of assumption-inference, and he or she must not be distracted by any task that can be routinized. In sum, the questionnaire protects the larger structure and objectives of the interview so that the interviewer can attend to immediate tasks at hand.

It is important to emphasize that the use of the questionnaire does not preempt the "open-ended" nature of the qualitative interview. Within each of the questions, the opportunity for exploratory, unstructured responses remains. Indeed, this opportunity is essential (Merton, Fiske, and Kendall, 1956: 43-50). Extemporaneous strategies of investigation are often the only road to understanding. The interviewer must be able to take full advantage of the contingency of the interview and pursue any opportunity that may present itself. In sum, the questionnaire that is used to order data and free the interviewer must not be allowed to destroy the elements of freedom and variability within the interview.

Furthermore, it is not the purpose of a fixed interview to abolish the characteristic abundance and "messiness" of qualitative data. Qualitative analysis, as we shall see below, requires that the interviewer work with substantial chunks of data. Without data of this character, it is difficult to see which ideas "go" together in the mental universe of the respondent, or the "cultural logic" on which these ideas rest. For analytic purposes, it is necessary to capture not just ideas but also the context in which these ideas occur. This context is, in a manner of speaking, the small amount of seawater that keeps the catch alive.

Issue 8: The Investigator/Respondent Relationship

One of the important differences between most qualitative and quantitative research is that the former demands a much more complex relationship between investigator and respondent. This complexity raises several issues.

The first of these is simple: Who does the respondent think the investigator is? As sentient social actors, North American respondents use every available cue to categorize the investigator and the project. They judge the institutional affiliation of the investigator, the project description, and even his or her appearance, mode of dress, and patterns of speech (Denzin, 1978b; Strauss and Schatzman, 1955). This semiotic exercise can dramatically influence whether and how the respondent responds to the questions they are asked (Briggs, 1986; Williams, 1964). If the investigator does not carefully control these cues, they will confound the nature of the respondent's participation in the interview and the data he or she provide (Benney and Hughes, 1956; Cannell et al., 1968, 1979; Lerner, 1956; Stebbins, 1972; Strauss and Schatzman, 1955; Vidich, 1955; Vogt, 1956).

Some of the strategies are straightforward. In my own experience, the best manner in which to manipulate the presentation of self for interview purposes is to strike a balance between formality and informality for each of the media in question. A certain formality in dress, demeanor, and speech is useful because it helps the respondent cast the investigator in the role of a "scientist," someone who asks very personal questions out of not personal but professional curiosity. This formality also helps to reassure the respondent that the investigator can be trusted to maintain the confidentiality has been promised the respondent. A certain, balanced, informality is useful because it reassures the respondent that for all of his or her professional training, the investigator is not a cold, distant creature unacquainted with or indifferent to the complexities and difficulties of the respondent's lifeworld. Naturally, the formality-informality balance will have to be tuned up or down according to the particular demands of special contexts.[10]

The second compelling question is the reciprocal one: Who does the investigator think the respondent is? There is a group within the qualitative research community that wishes to make the respondent a kind of collaborator (e.g., Elden, 1981; Gross and Mason, 1953: 200; Reason and Rowan, 1981). This approach has the merit of encouraging fuller disclosure of research objectives, and this in turn helps to solve some of the ethical issues that surround qualitative work (Whittaker, 1981). It is also praiseworthy for methodological reasons insofar as it sometimes produces quite spectacular results, as the work of Whyte (1955) and Turner (1967) attests (see Campbell, 1955).

But there is something in the qualitative interview that argues against full collaboration. Certainly, the investigator must be careful to establish a relationship of substance, and some kind of "connection" with the respondent (Benney and Hughes, 1956; Geertz, 1979; Stebbins, 1972; Wax, 1952). But it is possible to go too far and allow the intimacy to obscure or complicate the task at hand. The most obvious danger is that the respondent who is given the terms and objectives of research is not likely to give fully spontaneous and unstudied responses. The respondent may prove overhelpful, and try to "serve up" what he or she thinks is wanted. Second, collaboration raises the possibility of what Miller has called "overrapport" (1952). Unambiguous social distance between respondent and interviewer is especially necessary when "tough" questions must be asked and "delicate" analyses undertaken. I, for one, have worked with respondents whose personal charm and social position might well have obscured aspects of a life that needed to be seen and commented upon unblinkingly (McCracken, 1986). Third, when the interview is relatively anonymous, the respondent is blessed with the opportunity for candor (of the sort that is said to flourish on airplanes). This opportunity grows less likely as a more substantial relationship is established. There are grounds, then, to doubt the wisdom of making the respondent a collaborator.

The respondent in a qualitative interview is subject to several risks. Participation in qualitative interviews can be time consuming, privacy endangering, and intellectually and emotionally demanding in ways that quantitative interviews rarely are. To make matters worse, it is difficult for many respondents to anticipate these dangers at the outset of the interview. Investigators must take pains to see that the respondent is not overtly or subtly victimized by the interview process. The "standard ethics protocol" presented in Appendix B suggests one of the ways respondent rights can be protected.

But I am persuaded that the long interview offers the respondent benefits as well as risks. When I proposed long interviews with individuals between the ages of 65 and 75, funding agencies expressed concern that these interviews might prove fatiguing. I, too, was alarmed that my respondents might be dangerously taxed by the experience of answering intimate questions over a long period. Our fears proved unfounded. Almost without exception, respondents proved more durable and energetic than their interviewer. Again and again, I was left clinging to consciousness and my tape recorder as the interview was propelled forward by respondent enthusiasm. Something in the interview process proved so interesting and gratifying that it kept replenishing respondent energy and involvement.

The answers to this mystery are several. As Cannell and Axelrod (1956) and Caplow (1956) note, the qualitative interview gives the respondent the opportunity to engage in an unusual form of sociality.

Suddenly, they find themselves in the presence of the perfect conversational partner, someone who is prepared to forsake his or her own "turns" in the conversation and listen eagerly to anything the respondent has to say (Stebbins, 1972). This characteristic of the qualitative interview leads to other benefits, including the opportunity to make oneself the center of another's attention (Ablon, 1977; Von Hoffman and Cassidy, 1956), to state a case that is otherwise unheard (Leznoff, 1956; Wax, 1952), to engage in an intellectually challenging process of self-scrutiny (Merton and Kendall, 1946), and even to experience a kind of catharsis (Gorden, 1956: 159). Together, these advantages suggest that there are for most respondents benefits to compensate for the risks of the qualitative interview.

Issue 9:   Multimethod Approaches

The long qualitative interview for the study of contemporary North America should not be used in isolation. For all its perspicuity in certain matters, it is a perfectly unreliable, even misleading, guide in other respects. Or, to put this another way, the realities that the long qualitative interview can report are not the only realities with which the social scientist must contend (Trow, 1957: 35). Within the qualitative domain, there are several options at the investigator's disposal. Each of these have certain advantages. When some kind of participant observation is possible, it has dramatic advantages, as the anthropological investigator is well aware. It can deliver data that are beyond the conscious understanding or implicit grasp of even the best intentioned respondent. Indeed, it is in some cases the only way to obtain reliable data.[11] Focus groups can also be useful, particularly when respondents promise to be more forthcoming with the stimulus or the safety of a group of fellow respondents.[12] When the research project demands more rigor in the investigation of matters of belief and action than the long interview can provide, "repertory grid" analysis may be useful.[13] Research objectives may also call for life histories,[14] case studies,[15] protocols,[16] and the diary method.[17]

The qualitative researcher must also be prepared to take full advantage of quantitative methodologies. As it now stands, many qualitative researchers are disinclined to use quantitative methods. There is no question, however, that, especially in highly heterogeneous, complex societies, these methods are indispensable. Unfortunately, the literature that demonstrates how this most difficult of multimethod bridges can be constructed is not abundant.[18]

These nine issues are germane to every qualitative researcher. They have a particular relevance for the investigator who wishes to do qualitative research in his or her own society. Each of them represents another aspect of a great methodological challenge: How can one do qualitative research in a society that consistently frustrates the investigator's full and intimate access to the lives of his or her respondents. The next section of the book seeks to systematize the points made here, and to offer a model of inquiry for the long interview.

3. THE FOUR-STEP METHOD OF INQUIRY

For purposes of exposition, this section divides the circle of qualitative methods in two directions. The east-west axis separates two domains: analytic data and cultural data. The north-south axis separates two domains: review processes and discovery processes. Together, the axes divide the qualitative research circle into four quadrants, each of which represents a separate and successive step in the research process. The quadrants are:

(1) review of analytic categories and interview design
(2) review of cultural categories and interview design
(3) interview procedure and the discovery of cultural categories
(4) interview analysis and the discovery of analytical categories

These stages can be organized into a "four-step" pattern that shows their sequence and the nature of their interaction.

Step 1: Review of Analytic Categories

The first step of the long qualitative interview begins with an exhaustive review of the literature. Some researchers have taken qualitative methods as license to ignore the scholarship that bears on their investigation. They contend that qualitative methods are so powerfully and uniquely illuminating that they take the investigator

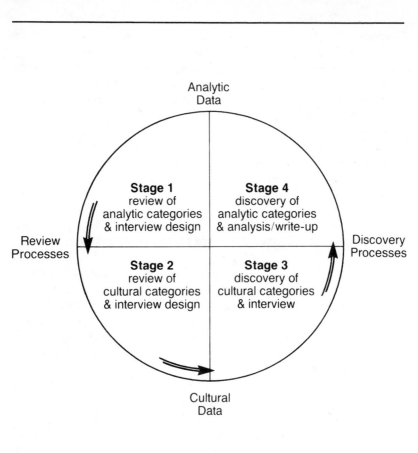

Analytic
Data

Stage 1
review of
analytic categories
& interview design

Stage 4
discovery of
analytic categories
& analysis/write-up

Review
Processes

Discovery
Processes

Stage 2
review of
cultural categories
& interview design

Stage 3
discovery of
cultural categories
& interview

Cultural
Data

Figure 1: Long Qualitative Interview: Four-Part Method of Inquiry

"where no one has gone before." This, they contend, makes the existing literature an irrelevance (and, at worst, a positivistic distortion). This strategy may well be ill advised. It denies qualitative researchers the benefit of previous research, and threatens to isolate them from the scholarly community. The only ghettos qualitative researchers have to fear in the present day are those they create for themselves.

A good literature review has many obvious virtues. It enables the investigator to define problems and assess data. It provides the concepts on which percepts depend. But the literature review has a special importance for the qualitative researcher. This consists of its ability to sharpen his or her capacity for surprise (Lazarsfeld, 1972b). The investigator who is well versed in the literature now has a set of expectations the data can defy. Counterexpectational data are conspicuous, readable, and highly provocative data. They signal the existence of unfulfilled theoretical assumptions, and these are, as Kuhn (1962) has noted, the very origins of intellectual innovation. A thorough review of the literature is, to this extent, a way to manufacture distance. It is a way to let the data of one's research project take issue with the theory of one's field.

It is, however, also true to say that preconceptions can be the enemy of qualitative research. As we have noted in the preceding section, it is easy for the researcher to take for granted the very things that are supposed to be the object of research. Some are even prepared to argue that a literature review creates preconceptions, and should therefore be avoided (Rennie et al., in press). But the benefits of the "preconceptions" that spring from the literature review are, perhaps, much greater than their costs. Or, to put this another way, a good literature review creates much more distance than it collapses.

Literature reviews, after all, are not simple exercises in idea collection. They are also critical undertakings in which the investigator exercises a constant skepticism. They are, in fact, a kind of qualitative analysis. They search out the conscious and unconscious assumptions of scholarly enterprises. They determine how these assumptions force the definition of problems and findings. The good literature review is a critical process that makes the investigator the master, not the captive, of previous scholarship.

The second purpose of the literature review is to aid in the construction of the interview questionnaire. It begins to establish the domain the interview will explore. It specifies categories and relationships that may organize the data. It helps to indicate the larger factors that direct respondent testimony. It helps to determine what the respondent should ask about and what he or she should listen for. By the end of the review, the investigator should have a list of topics for which questions must be prepared.

In sum, the first step of the four-step method of inquiry offers both a review and a "deconstruction" of the scholarly literature. It establishes a first survey of the ground upon which the interview will be conducted. It establishes an inventory of the categories and relationships that the interview must investigate.

Step 2:   Review of Cultural Categories

The second step of the qualitative circle consists in the review of cultural categories.[19] This is where the investigator begins the process of using the self as an instrument of inquiry. We have noted above that deep and long-lived familiarity with the culture under study has, potentially, the grave effect of dulling the investigator's powers of observation and analysis. But it also has the advantage of giving the investigator an extraordinarily intimate acquaintance with the object of study. This acquaintance gives the investigator a fineness of touch and delicacy of insight that few ethnographers working in other cultures can hope to develop. This is an exceptional analytic advantage and the long qualitative interview must be prepared to harness it as fully as possible. All of the remaining stages of the inquiry process are designed to do this, but the issue is especially pertinent in this second step.

The object of this step is to give the investigator a more detailed and systematic appreciation of his or her personal experience with the topic of interest. It calls for the minute examination of this experience. The investigator must inventory and examine the associations, incidents, and assumptions that surround the topic in his or her mind (Merton et al., 1956: 4). What is its place in daily life? Who does it involve, according to what schedules, for what putative and actual purposes, with which consequences? What assumptions about the world does the topic rehearse? How does it play out received understandings about how the world is constituted? The object is to draw out of one's own experience the systematic properties of the topic, separating the structural from the episodic, and the cultural from the idiosyncratic. One useful strategy here is to recall an incident in which the topic at hand was caught up in an episode dramatically at variance with one's previous experience and social convention. There is no better time to glimpse expectations and assumptions than when they are violated. The ordinary and taken-for-granted is thrown suddenly into relief (Agar, 1983a).

For a research project on the cultural properties of personal possessions and domestic space, my cultural review consisted of an examination of what I owned, how I had come to own it, how I would react to its loss. This led me to see that my own patterns of possession storage and display still reflect and declare a kind of "I'm not here for long" sentiment that survives my peripatetic youth. This, in turn, made me more sensitive to contrasting patterns of object storage and display on the part of my respondents.

I also examined my domestic circumstances, and this process lead me to see that in North American homes, kitchens and living rooms are almost always mediated by a dining room, or dining room space. As I thought about this it occurred to me that for the purposes of formal entertainment these three spaces are segregated into the following activity bundles: (1) food + no sociality (i.e., the kitchen), (2) food + sociality (i.e., the dining room/area), (3) sociality + no food (i.e., the living room). This made me more sensitive to how respondents conceived of domestic spaces and the nature of the sociality that took place within them.

There are three purposes to the cultural review. The first is to prepare for questionnaire construction. It is an opportunity to identify cultural categories and relationships that have not been considered by the scholarly literature. Once identified, these categories and relationships become the basis of question formulation. What should I look for? How will it be configured? What will be connected to what? What is the best and least obtrusive way to ask about it? And most important: What questioning strategy would most certainly elicit what I know about this subject?

The second purpose of this step is to prepare for the "rummaging" that will occur during data analysis. The interviewer examines cultural categories and their interrelationship, preparing the templates with which he or she will seek out "matches" in the interview data. The investigator listens to the self in order to listen to the respondent.

The third purpose of this strategy is to establish the "distance" that has been referred to throughout this book. Only by knowing the cultural categories and configurations that the investigator uses to understand the world is he or she in a position to root these out of the terra firma of familiar expectation. This clearer understanding of one's vision of the world permits a critical distance from it.

The second step of the "four-step" method seeks, then, to engage the investigator in two processes: familiarization and defamiliarization. Without the first, the listening skills needed for data collection and analysis are impoverished. Without the second, the investigator is not in a position to establish any distance from the his or her own deeply embedded cultural assumptions.

It is worth emphasizing that this cultural review is not feckless, dreamy introspection. Individuals raised in other research traditions are encouraged to treat their own experiences as bias and to set them aside. In the qualitative case, however, this material is the very stuff of understanding and explication. It represents vitally important intellectual capital without which analysis is the poorer.

With this review complete, an additional source of categories and relationships, this time cultural ones, have been identified and the inventory of these categories and relationships is now complete. It is now time to move to the third step, and the construction and implementation of the interview itself.

Step 3: Discovery of Cultural Categories

QUESTIONNAIRE CONSTRUCTION

Before the interview can begin, the questionnaire must be formalized. The first step is an easy one. It is the construction of a set of biographical questions with which to open the interview. These biographical questions, an example of which are given in Appendix A, allow the investigator to ascertain the simple descriptive details of an individual's life. Collecting these details in this way helps both to cue the interviewer to the biographical realities that will inform the respondent's subsequent testimony and to make sure that all of this material is readily at hand during analysis. Combing through interview testimony to work out biographical matters can be time consuming and difficult.

But genuinely qualitative questions are not so easily or mechanically identified. There are two general principles important to the remainder of the questionnaire construction. The first begins with the recognition that the first objective of the qualitative interview is to allow respondents to tell their own story in their own terms. The investigator seeks to keep as "low" and unobtrusive a profile as possible. In the case of question formulation, it is crucially important that questions be phrased in a general and nondirective manner. The objective here is to "spring" respondents, to move them to talk without overspecifying the substance or the perspective of this talk. In no instance may a question supply the terms of the answer it solicits. These opening, nondirective questions have been aptly named "grand-tour" questions (Spradley, 1979: 86-87; see Werner and Schoepfle, 1987: 318-343).

Once "grand-tour" testimony is forthcoming, it is relatively easy to sustain it in an unobtrusive way. The simplest way of doing so is through the use of "floating prompts" through the careful exploitation of several features of everyday speech (Churchill, 1973; Dohrenwend and Richardson, 1956). Simply raising one's eyebrow (the "eyebrow flash," as it is called in the paralinguistics literature) at the end of the respondent's utterance almost always prompts him or her to return to the utterance and expand upon it. A slightly more conspicuous device is simply to repeat the key term of the respondent's last remark with an interrogative tone. (Respondent: "So me and my girl friends decided to go out and get wrecked." Interviewer: "Wrecked?" Respondent: "Yeh, you know, really, really blasted.") If these techniques are not effective, the interviewer can be more forthcoming ("What do you mean 'blasted' exactly?") but not more obtrusive ("Do you mean 'intoxicated'?").

The object here is to watch for key terms (such as "wrecked" and "blasted") as they emerge from the testimony and to prompt the respondent to say more about them (Emerson, 1987: 75; Lazarsfeld, 1972a). Floating prompts allow this in a relatively unobtrusive, spontaneous way. Used in combination, grand-tour questions and floating prompts are sometimes enough to elicit all of the testimony the investigator needs. However, it is frequently the case that the categories that have been identified in the literature review and the cultural review do not emerge spontaneously in the course of the interview. In these cases, the investigator must be prepared to take a more "proactive," and obtrusive position. In these instances, the investigator must resort to "planned prompts."

Planned prompts are especially important when topics belong to the realm of the self-evident or the imponderable. The purpose of this second category of prompts is to give respondents something "to push off against." It is to give them an opportunity to consider and discuss phenomena that do not come readily to mind or speech. Perhaps the most important planned prompt is the "contrast" prompt (e.g., what is the difference between categories "x" and "y"?). These contrast questions should be restricted first to terms that the respondent has introduced. Only when these have been exhausted should the investigator introduce terms culled from the literature and cultural reviews. These planned prompts should be placed in the interview at the very end of each question category, so that they are not asked until, and unless, the material they are designed to elicit has failed to surface spontaneously.

Another planned prompting strategy is "category" questions. These are questions that allow the investigator to account for all of the formal characteristics of the topic under discussion. For instance, when what is being investigated is an activity or event, the investigator will want to determine how the respondent identifies each of its many aspects. Most of these will drift into the testimony in response to grand-tour questions, but many will go accidentally unconsidered. The investigator will want to know how the respondent defines the event's key actors, central action, dramatic structure, important props, necessary audience, ascribed roles, designated critics, social significance, cultural significance, and the consequences of good and bad performances. What does not emerge from grand-tour testimony must be gone after. (Naturally, the dramaturgical metaphor will be kept out of questions, and permitted into analysis only by written invitation.) Each topic category has a bundle of formal properties that must be anticipated in the construction of the questionnaire.

Another planned prompting strategy is to ask respondents to recall exceptional incidents in which the research topic was implicated. (The recitation of these incidents will sometimes surface on their own accord, and the investigator must be quick to develop them.) In these cases, a counterexpectational reality has already helped to pry the respondent away from his or her assumptions. What the investigator must do is to help the respondent report the results of this new distance. What was most striking about the incident? Why, precisely, was it surprising? What, exactly, did it contradict? Questions of these kind give the respondent an opportunity to glimpse expectations that are normally concealed from them. They also create new opportunities for the investigator. When the surface of social life is broken open by a "strange event," cultural categories and relationships prove suddenly visible.

A third planned prompting procedure is "auto-driving." This technique is highly obtrusive but, in some cases, extremely useful. The respondent is asked to comment on a picture, video, or some other stimulus, and to provide his or her own account of what they see there (e.g., Wax and Shapiro, 1956; Whyte, 1957). Normally, it is the investigator who prepares the stimulus material. In my own investigation of the cultural properties of North American homes, I have, for instance, used photographs showing different styles of interior design. These prompts proved provocative of useful data (McCracken, 1987, 1988a). A useful variation of this is to have the respondent prepare his or her own stimulus (a video of their homes, or a diary of their summer vacations, for instance) and then have them provide a commentary. Auto-driving is a useful prompting strategy because it helps to both foreground and objectify aspects of the respondents' experience that are otherwise difficult to bring into the interview.

Almost invariably the interview that satisfies these several conditions proves to be very long. In exploratory research, interview periods of two or three hours are common. The present author has been involved in six-hour interviews (divided into two three-hour or three two-hour segments), and the literature reports interviews as long as eight hours (Gross and Mason, 1953). Without long interview periods, it is impossible to let the respondent tell his or her own story and explore key terms in substantial chunks of unconstrained testimony. Happily, even respondents with dramatic constraints on their time prove willing to participate in these long interviews.

The final questionnaire, then, will consist in a set of biographical questions followed by a series of question areas. Each of these will have a set of grand-tour questions with floating prompts at the ready. It will also consist in planned prompting in the form of "contrast," "category," "special incident," and "auto-driving" questions. With this questionnaire in hand, the investigator has a rough travel itinerary with which to negotiate the interview. It does not specify precisely what will happen at every stage of the journey, how long each lay-over will last, or where the investigator will be at any given moment, but it does establish a clear sense of the direction of the journey and the ground it will eventually cover.

Choosing respondents is the final order of interview preparation. It has already been noted that these respondents are not a "sample," and that their selection should not be governed by sampling rules. There are, however, a few rules of thumb. Respondents should be perfect strangers (i.e., unknown to the interviewer and other respondents) and few in number (i.e., no more than eight). They should not have a special knowledge (or ignorance) of the topic under study. Most important, the selection of respondents is an opportunity to manufacture distance. This is done by deliberately creating a contrast in the respondent pool. These contrasts can be of age, gender, status, education, or occupation.

INTERVIEW PROCEDURE

Once the questionnaire is complete, the interview may begin in earnest. The opening of the interview has an important pragmatic burden. Whatever is actually said in the opening few minutes of the interview, it must be demonstrated that the interviewer is a benign, accepting, curious (but not inquisitive) individual who is prepared and eager to listen to virtually any testimony with interest. Understandably, respondents are not keen to reveal very much about themselves, or to take a chance with an idea, if there is any risk of an unsympathetic response (Rogers, 1945). Respondents must be assured that the potential loss-of-face that can occur in any conversation (and that we devote considerable energy and attention to avoiding in every conversation) is not a grave danger in the present one. The way in which to signal this benign attitude is to use the body postures and facial gestures that signal assent (Cannell and Axelrod, 1956; Palmer, 1928). It is better here to appear slightly dim and too agreeable than to give any sign of a critical or sardonic attitude.

The second way to create this atmosphere of face-safety is to make the opening questions simple, informational ones. A few minutes of idle chatter at this stage is welcome, for it gives the respondent a chance to see what the market will bear and what it will forgive (Berent, 1966). This is an important time to reassure the respondent because it is in these opening stages that he or she sets his or her defenses. The biographical data questions can serve this purpose.

Once the preliminaries are completed, the interviewer must deploy the grand-tour questions, and the "floating" and "planned" prompts. He or she must take care to see that data are collected for all of the categories and relationships that have been identified as important. But in addition to these categories and relationships, the respondent must also been prepared to identify and cultivate data on categories and relationships that have not been anticipated.

The interview is, in effect, the third source of information at the investigator's disposal. The literature review and the cultural review begin the search for categories and relationships. But, plainly, it is the interview itself that is the most important opportunity to pursue this search. It is also the most challenging. The respondent encounters salient data in the midst of a very crowded and complicated speech event. There is virtually no opportunity for unhurried identification or reflection. There is also the pressing knowledge that this opportunity will never come again. What the investigator does not capture in the moment will be lost forever. This is a challenging occasion because mistakes are both easy to make and impossible to rectify.

Capturing data on the wing, and capturing it whole, takes patience and care. The investigator must relinquish certain of his or her anxieties to the questionnaire, and let it guarantee the appearance of certain questions and the general character of the interview. What is required of the investigator within this structure is to listen with great care. It is a measure of the sheer difficulty of the listening process that qualitative interviewers frequently speak of the qualitative interview as being extraordinarily draining (even as many respondents, as we have noted, find it highly stimulating).[20]

The investigator is listening for many things. The first objective is key terms. When these terms appear in the testimony of the respondent, they must be patiently pursued. What are the assumptions, the companion terms, and the interrelationships of the term? The investigator listen for all of this, and when it is not forthcoming in response to grand-tour questions works out the logical possibilities, one by one, with the prompts at his or her disposal.

But the interviewer must also listen for many other things, including impression management, topic avoidance, deliberate distortion, minor misunderstanding, and outright incomprehension, taking, in each case, the necessary remedy to deal with the problem (Briggs, 1986; Douglas, 1976; Salamone, 1977). When the respondent is deliberately avoiding a topic, the strategy must be to see whether it can be approached more obliquely, or in terms of another, less threatening, idiom. In my own experience, I have observed respondents suddenly discover that they were saying more about themselves than they wanted to. In these cases, I seek to provide the respondent with a conversational gambit with which to change the topic. Politeness and strategy recommend this course. If the investigator insists on taking advantage of inadvertent testimony, the respondent is likely to respond by refusing any further intimacy.

It is also necessary to look down conversation avenues to glimpse what might lie ahead, and when the way appears blocked or unpromising, consider alternative strategies for getting at topics. This can be difficult. It may look, at first, that the respondent who has been asked to talk about his childhood home has changed the topic when he suddenly begins to talk about the baseball games he went to with his father. But one must let the respondent talk on for a moment. For what appears to be an abrupt change of topic may be a simple and important piece of clarification. In this case, home and baseball games may prove to be linked, because, for this respondent, home is mother's domain existing in contradistinction to father's world of sports. It is essential then to permit the respondent to follow his or her own lead.

It is also true, of course, that some respondents will jump topics with the frequency of a cheap phonograph needle. When respondents engage in "topic-splicing" and "topic-gliding" they must be gently returned to the topic of interest. This, too, should be done with only as much obtrusiveness as is absolutely necessary.

Finally, the interviewer must listen for implications and assumptions that will not come to the surface of the conversation by themselves, and think of ways of unearthing them. Some important data will never appear as such. The investigator can only know of their existence because they are indexed by the presence of other terms and meaning constellations. The careful listener must be listening not only for what exists in the interview but also what this material points to in the mind of the respondent. This is one of the most difficult strategies to formalize, for it comes usually in the form of an intuition. The investigator is suddenly aware that if the respondent thinks "x," he or she should also think "y."

In all this activity, the investigator must also remember to give the respondent plenty of room to talk. Once respondents have been brought within sight of the topic, they must be allowed to "go" wherever they wish. It is impossible to tell, in advance of careful analysis, whether (and how) what they are saying bears on the topic. The objective here is to generate enough testimony around these key terms that there will be sufficient data for later analysis. It is frequently only this subsequent period of reflection that will enable the investigator to see the connection and find the match.

It is sometimes difficult to elicit information in the quantity and the detail that is necessary for this subsequent analysis. A technique that can be useful for both the interviewer and the respondent is that of "playing dumb" (Becker, 1954). This is a variation on the calculated dimness referred to above. From the interviewer's point of view, the value of this strategy is that it helps to prevent glib assumptions. When the interviewer does not think in great leaps, it is easier to observe the small steps that make up the path of assumption. But this strategy also has a salutary effect on respondents. They respond with enthusiastic generosity when it appears the interviewer is not very worldly, knowing, or experienced; when he or she is a little "slow on the uptake." (Qualitative researchers who present themselves as university professors will find their respondents alarmingly quick to accept this self-characterization.) Respondents come to the investigator's aid with elaborate detail and exposition. They do so with the assurance that they will not be charged with belaboring the point—the penalty exacted in normal conversation. In my own case, I have encouraged respondents to give me an elementary treatment of the banking system (on the quite accurate grounds that this system is a perfect mystery to me) and have been rewarded with astonishingly useful (and bizarre) data.

In sum, the third step of the long qualitative interview consists of the careful construction of the questionnaire and the creation of biographical data questions, grand-tour questions, and "floating" and "planned" prompts, including in the latter category "contrast," "category," "special incident," or "auto-driving" strategies. The interview itself will open with a carefully contrived section in which respondent anxieties are laid to rest. The grand-tour questions and prompting strategies are then set in train and the interviewer must labor to identify key terms, minimize respondent distortion, choose the most promising avenues of inquiry, and listen for material that is indexed by respondent testimony but not made explicit in it. All of this activity must be set in a generous time-frame in order to let respondents tell their own story in their own terms.

Step 4: Discovery of Analytic Categories

The analysis of qualitative data is perhaps the most demanding and least examined aspect of the qualitative research process (Miles, 1979: 595; Piore, 1979). The following scheme intends to be mechanistic and indeterminate in roughly equal proportions. It prescribes a very particular scheme for the investigator to follow in the treatment of data. It suggests some very particular strategies for the consideration of this data. But it also leaves certain aspects of observation and analysis unspecified. The exact manner in which the investigator will travel the path from data to observations, conclusions, and scholarly assertion cannot and should not be fully specified. Different problems will require different strategies. Many solutions will be ad hoc ones.

There are several preliminary technical considerations to be dispatched. Interviews must be recorded on tape (and in some cases videotape). Interviewers who attempt to make their own record of the interview by taking notes create an unnecessary and dangerous distraction. A verbatim transcript of the interview testimony must be created. This transcript should be prepared by a professional typist using a transcribing tape recorder. Investigators who transcribe their own interviews invite not only frustration but also a familiarity with the data that does not serve the later process of analysis. Transcribers must be carefully cued and supervised so that the transcripts are indeed "verbatim" records, and not excerpted or summarized versions of the original tape. Transcription should take place on a word processor, so that both a hard copy version of the interview and a machine-readable file are created.

The object of analysis is to determine the categories, relationships, and assumptions that informs the respondent's view of the world in general and the topic in particular. The investigator comes to this undertaking with a sense of what the literature says ought to be there, a sense of how the topic at issue is constituted in his or her own experience, and a glancing sense of what took place in the interview itself. The investigator must be prepared to use all of this material as a guide to what exists there, but he or she must also be prepared to ignore all of this material to see what none of it anticipates. If the full powers of discovery inherent in the qualitative interview are to be fully exploited, the investigator must be prepared to glimpse and systematically reconstruct a view of the world that bears no relation to his or her own view or the one evident in the literature.

There are five stages to the analysis process. Each of them represents a higher level of generality. The first stage treats each utterance in the interview transcript in its own terms, ignoring its relationship to other aspects of the text. The treatment of each useful utterance creates an observation. The second stage takes these observations and develops them, first, by themselves, second, according to the evidence in the transcript, and, third, according to the previous literature and cultural review. The third stage examines the interconnection of the second-level observations, resorting once again to the previous acts of literature and culture review. The focus of attention has now shifted away from the transcript and toward the observations themselves. Reference to the transcript is now made only to check ideas as they emerge from the process of observation comparison. The fourth stage takes the observations generated at previous levels and subjects them, in this collective form, to collective scrutiny. The object of analysis is the determination of patterns of intertheme consistency and contradiction. The fifth stage takes these patterns and themes, as they appear in the several interviews that make up the project, and subjects them to a final process of analysis. These five stages are summarized in Figure 2.

This five-stage process inscribes a movement from the particular to the general. The investigator begins deeply embedded in the finest

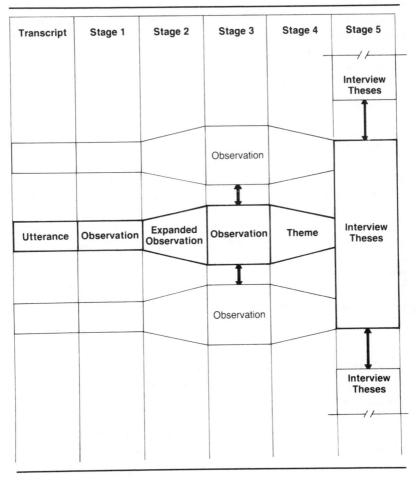

Figure 2: Long Qualitative Interview: Stages of Analysis

details of the interview transcript and, with each successive stage, moves upward to more general observations. Analytic advantages aside, this scheme has the additional virtue of creating a record of the processes of reflection and analysis in which the investigator engaged. Such a record has recently been identified as a condition of the qualitative reliability check (Kirk and Miller, 1986: 51), a matter to which we shall return in the next chapter.

In the first stage of analysis the investigator judges individual utterances with little concern for their larger significance. At this stage, what is important are the "intensive" relations of the utterance, the meanings contained within its range of implication. No attention should be paid to the utterance's "extensive" relations, the relationship its bears to other utterances. At this stage, the investigator acts much like an archaeologist, sorting out important material from unimportant material with no attention to how the important material will eventually be assembled.

The object of first-stage analysis is to see whether one can treat the utterance as an entranceway. One wants to go through the utterance into the assumptions and beliefs from which it springs (Geertz, 1976). There are several strategies that can be exercised here. The first stage of analysis consists of a "mannered" reading of the transcript. The investigator must put off "readerly" acts of meaning construction. He or she must come to the text with a certain disingenuous wonder, refusing to supply the assumptions and understandings with which we are normally so quickly and unconsciously forthcoming. It is useful, for instance, to take metaphors literally. When the respondent speaks of being "blasted," it is worth taking this figure of speech at its face. Is the person violently and suddenly destroyed by heavy drinking? Plainly not. Well, is the social person in some sense so destroyed? Perhaps so. If so, what does this tell us about the sensation and the intention of the act of "blasting"? Another strategy is to supply assumptions. If my respondent insists that "x" is "y," what else might he or she suppose about the world? If, for instance, drinking is an activity in which certain social conventions and creatures are destroyed, what does this tell me about the nature of the conventions and creatures, and the respondent's relation to them?

This is where the investigator must use the self as an instrument. The investigator must read interview testimony with a very careful eye both to what is in the data, and what the data "sets off" in the self. Attending to the self as carefully as to the data in the interview, the investigator will hear a stream of associations evoked by the stream of utterances. This associational activity is a treasure-trove of illumination. Again and again, the investigator recognizes what is being said, not because the utterance has been successfully decoded but because a sudden act of recognition has taken place. A little voice within the investigator says, "Oh, sure, I know what that is." Just as often, what the utterance activates is not the investigator's own experience but his or her imaginative capacity to glimpse the possibility of alien meanings. In this case the little voice says, "How interesting, it's almost as if he/she is saying. . . ." Carefully monitored, the associational activity of the self will deliver insights into the nature of the data. This "intuition," as it is sometimes called, is indeed the most powerful (if most obscure) of the analytic devices at our disposal (Berreman, 1966: 349).

This is also where the investigator uses the matches from the literature and culture reviews that were prepared in the first two stages of the research process. In this somewhat less obscure undertaking, the investigator takes the conclusions of the academic literature and culture review, using them as templates with which to search out the systematic properties of the interview data.

As the investigator works through the data, certain avenues that appear to go right to the heart of the matter will emerge. The parts of the interview that present themselves in this manner should be marked as such, but the investigator must resist the temptation to follow them and neglect other possibilities. Beware premature closure! The investigator must be prepared to postpone generalities for later stages of the analysis (Glaser and Strauss, 1965).

The second stage of analysis has three stages within it. The investigator continues to develop each observation created in the first stage. The object here is to extend the observation beyond its original form until its implications and possibilities are more fully played out. When this is complete, observations are related back to the transcript. Each observation is a kind of lens with which the transcript can be scanned to see whether any relationship or similarity suggests itself. When this is complete, the observations are examined, one in relation to the other. A keen eye must be kept for all logical relations, not only those of identity and similarity, but those of opposition and contradiction as well. All of the templates created at early stages of the research process should still be in play.

In the third stage, observations are once again developed on their own accord, and, now, in relation to other observations. By this time in the analytical process, the main focus of interest has shifted away from the main body of the transcript. Reference is now made to this transcript only to confirm or discourage developing possibilities. The object of study is the observations and the pieces of text from which they sprang. This examination of earlier observations will give rise to a further set of observations. By this time, a process of refinement should be taking place. A field of patterns and themes should be rising into view. Moreover, the field of constraint should now be richer and clearer. By this time, the investigator should be speculating in a better organized, more exacting context. As this speculation goes forward, general properties of the data should be emerging. The general outlines of the interview should now be apparent.

The fourth stage is a time of judgment. Some of the passages of the interview will by this time become surrounded by comments and these comments will have generated comments of their own. These coral-like formations are the place to which the investigator may return and sort out the general themes implicit there. What has been allowed to multiply profusely must now be harvested and winnowed. At this point the investigator is not thinking about how the general point bears on any of the other parts of the interview. He or she is working only within each formation to draw out and lay bare the general theme.

Once all the themes are identified in this manner, a decision must be made as to their interrelationship. Some of these themes will be redundant, and the best formulation should be chosen while the others are eliminated. The remainder can then be organized hierarchically. One or two themes will be the chief points under which the remainder of the themes can be subsumed. There will be a set of residual themes that remain. These are extremely important and valuable pieces of your argument. Observe carefully whether any of them contradict any of the themes that have been identified, or the hierarchy into which these themes have been organized. Those that are not useful in this way may be discarded.

The fifth stage calls for a review of the stage-four conclusions from all of the interviews that have been undertaken for a project. It is time to take the themes from each interview and see how these can be brought together into theses. It is here that a process of transformation takes place in which the cultural categories that have been unearthed in the interview become analytic categories. By this time one is no longer talking about the particulars of individual lives but about the general properties of thought and action within the community or group under study. Furthermore, one is no longer talking about the world as the respondent sees it. One is now talking about the world as it appears to the analyst from the special analytic perspective of the social sciences. Fully possessed of general and abstract properties, the investigator's observations are now "conclusions" and ready for academic presentation.

STEP 4 AND THE USE OF COMPUTER TECHNOLOGY

There is a simple way of mechanizing the five-stage process through the use of computer technology. In this method, the investigator examines the transcript with a personal computer and word processing software. When an observation suggests itself, the investigator types this observation directly into the transcript immediately following the utterance that inspired it. Sophisticated word processing programs, such as Microsoft Word and Word Perfect, allow the investigator to mark these inserted passages and to suppress them easily in screen, disk, or print versions of the file. This gives the investigator access to both the pristine text and a record of his or her observations situated in the text exactly where they suggested themselves.

The first stage of analysis will leave the investigator with the original transcript and a set of observations. The next stage of analysis examines the first set of observations in situ and inserts the meta-observations they inspire alongside them in the transcript. To prepare for the third and fourth stages, however, it is worthwhile to take advantage of the "mark and copy" functions of the word processor, copying all of the observations and the utterances that occasioned them into a new file. This represents a great act of reduction. It removes from consideration all parts of the transcript that have not given rise to an observation, and leaves the investigator with a much simpler record for third-stage analysis. Using this new file only, the investigator generates the next set of observations and records them in the file. The original transcript is now only consulted when some special point must be clarified. (This is easily done with the word processing program that allows split-screen access to two files simultaneously.) For the fourth stage, an entirely new file may be created that is then filled with the most general points that have emerged in the foregoing analysis. This file should be a tidy package of limited themes. The final stage calls for the creation of a file that contains the fourth-stage treatments from each interview.

It is worth adding here that computers can also make themselves useful as a means of searching interview transcripts. It is possible, for instance, to ask the computer to identify every passage in the interview testimony in which two words, or word clusters, appear within a specified number of words from one another. For example, the computer can identify all of the passages in which the word "father," "dad," "my old man," "pop," or "papa" appears within, say, 15 words of the word "holidays," "camping," "summer," "vacation," "the camper," or "the cottage." This possibility should open up certain interesting observational strategies for those who have their interviews transcribed to a machine-readable file. On the whole, I have preferred the more "organic" approach suggested in this book, treating passages as they appear in the interview text. But I have used the index and search software program called "Zyindex" for "final check" purposes to ensure I have not neglected a key passage.[21]

As a final point, this account of the long qualitative interview has assumed that data collection and analysis will take place in two separate and successive stages. This approach is especially useful when the research objective has a relatively narrow focus. However, when research objectives are somewhat more general, it is sometimes useful to resort to a "tiered" pattern of interviews. In this case, the investigator interviews respondents in successive groups. After the first group is interviewed, data analysis is undertaken in order to narrow objectives and refine questions. The second group is then interviewed, and a further narrowing and refinement takes place. The final set of interviews is permitted to inquire about very particular matters. This design strategy is especially useful when qualitative methods are being used for "exploratory" purposes. But it has the additional virtue of allowing data collection and analysis to intermingle. Glaser and Strauss (1965) suggest that this intermingling (which occurs naturally in participation observation projects) is an aid to analysis, giving the investigator an opportunity to engage in a process of "constant comparison."

In sum, the final step of the long qualitative interview calls for the careful verbatim transcription of interview data. Working with the data in this form, the investigator undertakes five stages of analysis. The first of these locates the investigator securely in the fine details of the interview, while the last advances him or her to general scholarly conclusions. In this ascent, the investigator moves from data to observations and from these to meta-observations and from these to still more general observations, keeping a careful eye throughout on the data, the observations, and the literature and culture reviews. At each stage investigators employ what they know about the topic at hand, even as they glimpse possibilities that are entirely new to them. Thus do the cultural categories of the interview data become analytic categories and assume the character of formal scholarly conclusions.

4. QUALITY CONTROL

How does the investigator ensure the quality of his or her own qualitative research? How does the user of this research treat it with confidence? These are questions to which there are still only general and imprecise answers. This chapter suggests one of the strategies by which quality may be assessed.

Much of the difficulty surrounding this question stems from the tendency to judge qualitative research by quantitative standards. As we noted above in our discussion of Issue 3, it is important to keep the distinction between qualitative and quantitative research visible and clear. In the first, categories take shape in the course of research, whereas in the second, they are fixed from the beginning. In the first, the analyst uses his or her methods to capture complexity and to search out patterns of interrelationship between many categories. In the second, the analyst looks, instead, for a very precise relationship between a limited set of categories. The first is designed to elicit testimony that the respondent has difficulty articulating with ease and clarity. The second seeks to ask different, more precisely answerable, questions. In the first, the investigator is an instrument of investigation. In the second, the investigator is the deliberately dispassionate operator of a piece of finely calibrated methodological machinery. Finally, the qualitative tradition offers explanations that take us "back stage" in the culture in question, to let us glimpse assumptions and categories that are otherwise hidden from view. It is not intended to capture issues of distribution and generalization. It tells us what people think and do, not how many of them think and do it.

As thoroughgoing, dramatic, and obvious as this difference is, many social scientists periodically forget themselves, and apply quantitative standards to qualitative inquiry. This is mistaken but not entirely surprising. For the qualitative traditions have not developed all the quality controls they might have. This is one of the key points on which they have not quite yet put their house in order. My suggestion, following the inspiration of Evans-Pritchard (1961: 26), is that we take the conservative course and ally ourselves with the research communities that have the longest and most distinguished qualitative research tradition. I suggest that we should turn to the humanities and adopt their standards of interpretation and quality control.

The research traditions in the humanities are all long practiced in the judgment of interpretive efforts and materials. While theoretical orientations come and go, there is a extrasystemic and logical foundation for the evaluation of what is good and what is bad explanation. Indeed, theoretical orientations come and go precisely because a new perspective or "paradigm" is seen to satisfy the conditions of explanation more powerfully than previous ones. The language of this critical tradition is strange to positivist ears. This language asks how "illuminating," "encompassing," and "elegant" an argument is. When the data are especially complex, contradictory, or unclear, the terms "supple," "adroit," and "cunning" are also used.

Positivists delight in scorning the apparent imprecision of this standard. But they do not seem to realize that this position makes them de facto critics of extraordinary accomplishments in the fields of history, philosophy, English literature, art history, and the classics. It is worth observing that none of these fields demonstrates an inability to discriminate between good and bad scholarship. Indeed, all of them make these discriminations with an enviable fineness.

Unfortunately, there is no single source to which we can turn for a summary statement of the research standards in the humanities. I have taken the liberty of trying to create such a statement myself. Ironically, I have found the scheme proposed by Bunge (1961) for the assessment of scientific theory the most useful frame with which to work. The version of the scheme presented here is edited so that it is suitable for the evaluation of explanation instead of theory, and qualitative instead of quantitative inquiry. In a summary form, then, an explanation of qualitative data must exhibit the following conditions or (as Bunge calls them) "symptoms of truth":

1. It must be exact, so that no unnecessary ambiguity exists.
2. It must be economical, so that it forces us to make the minimum number of assumptions and still explain the data.
3. It must be mutually consistent, so that no assertion contradicts another.
4. It must be externally consistent, so that it conforms to what we independently know about the subject matter.
5. It must be unified, so that assertions are organized in a manner that subsumes the specific within the general, unifying where possible, discriminating when necessary.
6. It must be powerful, so that it explains as much of the data as possible without sacrificing accuracy.
7. It must be fertile, so that it suggests new ideas, opportunities for insight.[22]

These standards are vital to the evaluation of any formal explanation. But they are especially crucial to qualitative inquiry, in which there is no realistic opportunity for the replication and confirmation that exists in the natural sciences. The first condition, exactness, requires that an explanation be stated as precisely as possible so that the reader is left in no reasonable doubt as to what is intended. Imprecision does more than merely hobble the explanation. It also has the unhappy effect of making it impossible for the evaluator to determine whether any of the other truth symptoms have been satisfied.

The second, economy, says that an explanation must not force us to make unnecessary assumptions. This is where "elegance" becomes a consideration. Inelegant explanations are those that are structurally redundant. They require more foundational materials than are absolutely necessary. From an architectural point of view, the uneconomical explanation is a badly built explanation.

The third condition, mutual consistency, demands that the body of assertions that make up the explanation not interfere with one another. Assertions can serve to establish their own demanding context, so that the investigator is not able to introduce new assertions unless and until these can be made to square with the existing ones. Some fail to allow assertions to perform this quality check, and mutual consistency then becomes the ground for criticism. In the later stages of analysis, this condition forces the investigator to ask whether new ideas and insights square with previous ones and how they do so, and then to observe how the entire structure of the explanation would have to change to accommodate them.

The fourth condition, external consistency, is a tricky one. What is being asked here is not that an explanation conforms to everything else we know about a topic. This "strong" form of the condition would effectively prevent every kind of intellectual innovation. What is called for is a more discriminating vigilance on the part of the investigator, one that ensures that an explanation is consistent with most of the important guiding principles of their social scientific style of inquiry. The principle of reflection must be, "Does this conform to what I otherwise think about cultural and social phenomena?" But even here one must be careful. As Kuhn (1962) has told us, it is precisely the data that refuse to submit to our guiding paradigms that offer (when differently construed) the hope of important theoretical advances. External consistency is an important condition, but it must be used judiciously.

The fifth condition, unity, holds that the explanation must not exist simply as a serial chain of assertions, but as a set of organized and interrelated ideas. Some assertions, on careful inquiry, will be seen to be mere instances of some others and they should be so subsumed. Other assertions will appear to exist in a relationship of contradiction to other assertions. In this case the explanation must explain one of the assertions away or bifurcate to accommodate them both. This too is a matter of good intellectual architecture. Having given the explanation strong foundations by satisfying the second condition, the investigator must now give it a clear, balanced, and harmonious structure by satisfying the present one.

The sixth condition, power, calls for an explanation that explains as much of the ethnographic data as possible without the compromise of undue specificity. The evaluator must ask, "Is there any way of explaining these data that is more comprehensive but not more complicated?" The power of an explanation is its ability to do more with less.

The seventh condition, fertility, is really a measure of whether the explanation of a particular project has any value outside of this narrow context. The question here is, "Does this explanation help me to see the world more clearly? Does it give me a lens with which to examine the world?" It is the objective of every piece of qualitative inquiry to capture not just the particular but also the general properties of human discourse. This makes fertility an important measure of the "goodness" of an explanation.

Taken together, these "symptoms of truth" are one of the ways the quality of a qualitative exercise may be evaluated. As a standard, it does not demand that explanations be "true." Nor does it demand that any particular theoretical perspective be adopted. It demands merely that they exhibit the characteristics of good intellectual craftsmanship. These may not fully satisfy our wish for certainty. But they will go a very long way toward allowing us to sort the sheep from the goats, and for present purposes this is enough.

5. THE WRITING-UP PROCESS

Writing up the results of qualitative research can be difficult. To exploit the full powers of insight and illumination that reside in the qualitative interview, the investigator has properly allowed the respondents to generate a great deal of detailed and diverse testimony. But this now becomes a mass of complex data that must be winnowed and organized into the narrow confines of a 30- or 40-page paper.[23]

The good news is that most of the work of creating a paper is already accomplished. By identifying, organizing, and interrelating themes and theses in the last step of the interview, the investigator has isolated the substance of the paper. Most of the work that remains is the laborious process of herding these observations and insights into a single pasture.[24]

There are two important forms of the write-up. The first is used when a very specific topic of research has been chosen by a third party and assigned to the investigator. This occurs when a government agency, private company, or course instructor sets the topic of research. The second is used when the investigator does not have a specific set of objectives but has been prompted by curiosity or an external agent to investigate a general topic. These two quite different projects call for quite different write-up strategies. Let us take each of them in turn.

Assigned-Topic Write-Up

The first objective of the write-up is to construct an introduction. For the qualitative researcher working on an assigned topic, this introduction is relatively straightforward. Let us suppose that the assigned topic calls for the qualitative investigation of the time management patterns of single parents and the implications of these patterns for a federal day-care policy. This research mandate establishes the terms of the introduction. Here is a typical introductory paragraph for such a paper:

> How single parents organize their day is a matter of interest to social scientists and policymakers alike. The present paper offers the results of a qualitative investigation of this compelling topic. The first section of the paper will review the previous literature on the topic. The second will give an ethnographic picture of how some single parents see and structure their daily lives. The third section of the paper offers a formal identification of the time management objectives of these parents and the alternative strategies by which they pursue them. The final part of the paper will discuss the policy implications of these observations and, more specifically, the ways in which this information might be applied in the creation of a federal day-care policy.

The next section is the literature review. It is time to circle back to the review that was performed for the first step of the long interview. Do the themes and theses confirm the way in which people have framed the study of this issue in previous literature? Do they confirm their findings and their conclusions? In this case, the literature review should deftly summarize this scholarship and note how the present paper will help confirm, extend, and refine it. Do the themes and theses lead the investigator into areas unexplored by the existing literature? In this case, the review should summarize the literature, observe the topics and perspectives it has neglected, and then note how the paper will treat these topics. Do the themes and theses contradict the findings and perspectives of the literature? In this event, the review should summarize the literature and then show how the data encourage a different perspective and set of conclusions. Some literature reviews will be a combination of all three of these possibilities, but only one of them is necessary.

Let us suppose that in our hypothetical study of time management, we observed that previous studies (1) have treated single parents as rational decision makers for whom all time units are equal and to be apportioned according to the same maximizing logic, (2) have noted that the single-parent-child relationship is charged with particular qualities of anxiety, and (3) have neglected to consider the particular patterns of parent-child interaction that exist in the single-parent home. In this case, our literature review will note each of these characteristics, promising to contradict the first, extend the second, and correct the third.

The second section of the paper is designed to take advantage of the fact that qualitative research can take the reader into the mind and the life of the respondent. This section should give the reader a guided tour of these terrains by choosing sample quotes that capture the ideas and concerns of the single parent. Here is an example of a rich and useful quote culled from our hypothetical interview.

> Morning is our most important time. I'm fresh, Jenny is fresh, and we just seem to really click somehow. Jenny helps me make the breakfast and we sit and talk . . . what happened yesterday, what's going to happen today, general stuff. Then the day starts and we go our separate ways. And, boy, do we get separated! I mean, physically and emotionally. By the time I pick her up after work we're tired and irritable and played out. At least I am anyhow . . . and she is too, sometimes.

It is not necessary to frame these quotes very exactly. For the purposes of this section it is enough to say something general. The quote above can be introduced with a simple descriptive statement (e.g., "Single parents spoke with intensity about the difficulties imposed on the family by the demands of the larger world."). Remember formal analysis has not yet begun. The object is merely to introduce the reader to interview material.

It is time now to undertake the third section and a formal treatment of your observations and conclusions. You will want to return to the literature review and introduction, and determine the best way to present findings. In the case of our examples, three subsections may be appropriate, each with its own subheading. These would consist of the following:

3.1 Concepts of time and patterns of activity for the single-parent family. This section will repeat what has been said in the literature review: that previous studies have treated the single parent as an individual who treats time as a uniform resource. It would then argue that project data suggest that not all time units in the day have the same significance for the single parent. As a result, there are constraints on how parents apportion their time. For some parents, the key time of the day is the morning, the time when crucial family rituals and interactions take place. For others, the crucial time is evening, when other rituals are played out. For others, lunch time is the key moment of interaction. The investigator may wish to observe the significance of these moments of family interaction, and how and why they should be so closely tied to particular times of the day. This discussion should be rooted in the ethnographic particulars of the interview data but working always to generalize so that section addresses the formal properties of the family's time management patterns.

3.2 The single-parent-child relationship. This section will rehearse the salient literature, noting that the present study also found this relationship to be charged with anxiety, as single parents worry about the development of a child who must spend so much time away from home. This is an opportunity to explore the precise nature of this anxiety and to show some of its formal properties by exploring the data. Even when the investigator finds him- or herself concurring with previous scholarship, it is still possible to make an important contribution to it by using the data to illuminate, explore, and refine the terms and relationships that appear there.

3.3 Family rituals and the single-parent family. This section notes that the literature has failed to observe that time in single-parent households often contains and is organized by certain family rituals (e.g., watching special programs together, making meals together, "putting to bed" rituals, or "lunch time"). This is your opportunity to reveal the existence of these rituals, describe them so that their formal properties are clear, and then discuss their implications for the nature of the relationship between parent and child in a single-parent family.

The last section of the paper considers how the findings can best be applied in the creation of public policy. It will observe that time management is not an abstract calculation for the single parent and that certain times of the day have special significance for parent-child interaction. It might recommend a flexible schedule that lets some parents bring in and pick up their children early while others bring in and pick up their children late. This is the place to observe that this flexible scheduling would do something to address the special anxieties felt by the single parent and allow for key patterns of interaction. The larger implications, costs, and difficulties of such a scheduling pattern must also be explored.

In sum, there are several clear-cut stages to the write-up process: introduction, literature review, ethnographic picture, formal discussion, policy implications. This process bears some resemblance to landing a plane. The introduction takes place at a very high altitude from which the entire terrain is visible. The literature review bring the plane down to within view of the airport and a more particular view of the world below. The ethnographic picture represents touchdown. Having surveyed the terrain from a general perspective and identified the landing strip, the paper puts its wheels down on the terra firma of ethnographic data. But this landing does not complete the journey. After a brief taxi over the landing strip, the plane takes off again. With the formal discussion it returns to a high altitude so that the larger significance and formal properties of the earth below are once again visible. The discussion of policy takes the plane higher still, so that the terrain can be seen in relation to the entire landscape. Controlling these levels of generality and accomplishing flawless touchdowns and takeoffs are the real challenges of the writing-up process.

Open-Topic Write-Up

Writing an introduction for a more exploratory project is less easy. There is no research directive to specify what the paper should accomplish. It is necessary for the author to fashion his or her own terms of reference. To do so, it is necessary to gather the themes and theses identified in Step 4 of the long interview process and circle back to Step 1 of the process. Is there agreement between one's findings and those of the literature? Are there differences? The answer to these questions provides the introduction to the paper.

Let us suppose that the purpose of the qualitative study was the investigation of how adolescents think about fast food, how it fits into their notions of nutrition and health, and how it fits into their eating and social patterns. In order to prepare the write-up, we return to Step 4 and collect the themes and theses that we created in the final stage of analysis.

With this material in mind, we circle back to Step 1 and see whether our results confirm or disconfirm what the literature says about adolescents and fast-food eating patterns. Let us suppose that while previous research correctly anticipated several reasons why teenagers should like fast-food outlets, it entirely ignored a crucial one: that for some teenagers fast-food consumption is not so much a matter of nutrition as sociality. Our (hypothetical) research tells us that the reason some teenagers go to local fast-food outlets is to meet friends, catch up on gossip, to watch one another interact, and only secondarily and incidentally to eat. The fast-food outlet has become a kind of community center for this group. The opening paragraph for such a write-up might be the following:

> The relationship between fast-food outlets and the eating habits of the North American teenager is the subject of a growing body of social scientific scholarship. This scholarship tells us that teenagers have become frequent and intensive users of fast-food outlets for several reasons: to replace meals no longer prepared in the home, to establish an independence from the home, to have time enough for new levels of social, athletic, or academic activity. The present study is prepared to support all of these contentions, but it wishes also to add a neglected factor: that teenagers patronize fast-food outlets for social reasons and that fast-food outlets are important centers for their social lives. This argument will be made in three stages. The paper will offer a review of the literature, an ethnographic glimpse of the fast-food outlet as social center, and a formal review of patterns of sociality that exist there.

These three sections of the paper can be written as they are for the assigned-topic write-up described above. The review will deftly block out the several conclusions of the literature, and then observe that the scholarship has neglected one important factor.

The ethnographic picture will take readers into the fast-food outlet, and let them see and hear the teenagers who meet there. Why do they come? How long do they stay? Where do they sit? With whom do they sit? What do they talk about? What do they eat? Why would a community center, laundromat, or "greasy spoon" not serve the same purpose? At what point in their development do they cease to use the fast-food outlet as a social center and why? The investigator should try to answer these questions in the language of the respondent. The reader will be able to glimpse conclusions in the data, but for the moment they are being given merely a quick and general tour.

The last section will systematically and formally examine how the fast-food outlet serves as a center for the social lives of these teenagers. What is required here is a treatment of what kinds and patterns of sociality take place in the fast-food outlet. What makes the outlet so appropriate as a place for this sociality? How do these patterns of sociality encourage or discourage different patterns of nutrition? The investigator should try to answer these questions in a manner that captures as many of the particular details as possible in as economical and elegant a manner as possible.

In sum, these two write-up forms suggest only two of the ways the investigator may wish to present the results of ethnographic inquiry. There are two important objectives to keep in mind as other formats are explored and developed. One of these may be called the "herding" objective: to allow rich and abundant data to speak to the reader without losing the writer's or the reader's way in a mass of ethnographic detail. The second may be called the "landing" objective: to provide a clear and vivid sense of the ethnographic particulars while also showing the general formal properties and theoretical significance of these data.

6. MANAGING QUALITATIVE RESEARCH

In some qualitative traditions, a single individual is expected to design the research project and perform all phases of data collection, analysis, and publication. The anthropologist who goes off to the field alone is necessarily called upon to act in this classic "one-man-band" capacity.

Most social scientific research, however, has a more complicated division of labor. In some cases, the individual who conceives of the research will never actually participate in it. As a research manager, he or she will direct and commission some set of individuals to undertake the research. In other cases, the individual is part of a research team. Sometimes this is a group of social scientists; sometimes it is a single social scientist surrounded by a group of professional researchers and/or graduate students. Quite different strategies are needed for managing these two quite different research configurations.

Commissioned Research

Let us first consider the individual who is concerned with distant management of qualitative research. This individual can be the research manager (i.e., project director) of a large omnibus project or the party charged with commissioning single, purpose-built pieces of ad hoc research. There are four important issues for this manager.

The first of these is the conceptualization of the research project. The research manager must be absolutely certain that he or she wants qualitative research for the right reasons. It is sometimes the case that managers use qualitative methods because they do not know quantitative methods, because they imagine qualitative methods are a cheap substitute for quantitative methods, or because they are naively prepared to reach quantitative conclusions on the basis of qualitative study. As I argue above, qualitative data and conclusions should never be made to serve as a substitute for quantitative ones. It is also true that qualitative data properly collected are almost always more expensive and time consuming than quantitative data. Furthermore, it is, as I have noted above, almost always messier, less certain data.

As a rule of thumb, then, the research manager should treat quantitative methods as the default method. The question to ask is this: "Can I answer my questions using quantitative methods, or does the nature of my project require me to use qualitative methods?" The presumption of utility should always lie with the quantitative methods. More bluntly: Do not use qualitative methods unless you cannot use quantitative ones.

The reason the manager will find him- or herself required to use qualitative methods is when he or she suspects that the issue at hand turns in some important way on the ways in which individuals conceive of, or construe, their world. If, for instance, the issue is how people see the museum as a source of entertainment and instruction, then qualitative methods are obligatory. But if the only real issue is the price-point beyond which museum admission cannot climb, then there is no need for qualitative research.

The real nature of the difficulty here is that the manager cannot know what he or she does not know. To put this another way, the manager may be using a term or concept that he or she takes utterly and invisibly for granted. Respondents also use the term, also take it for granted, but, unlike the manager, they attach their own, quite different meaning to it. Frequently, this difference in usage goes undetected because it never occurs to the manager that such a difference could conceivably exist. A good example here is the manager who commissioned quantitative research to determine the significance of candy in the food habits of a group of respondents. To everyone's surprise, the survey captured nothing about candy. Subsequent inquiry revealed that these respondents did not define candy as a "food" on the (mistaken) grounds that it does not have nutritional value.

It is difficult, then, for managers to be certain that they do not need to use qualitative researchers. The first and second stages of the interview process are one way to manufacture distance and unearth assumptions. There are some managers who use "entry" interviews and focus groups at the very beginning of the project to see whether respondents use the same terms and concepts. They will then use "exit" interviews at the end of the project to check their inferences and plans in the same way for the same reason.

In many cases these entry and exit checks will be unnecessary, especially where the manager is very familiar with the research ground. (This should be a familiarity that rests on qualitative work and not simply long-standing acquaintance with the area of research. Long-standing acquaintance is one of the favorite hiding places for the unexamined assumption.) Normally, it should be enough to do the literature and culture reviews. As long as the manager is prepared to glimpse the fact that the world is differently configured from the one he or she inhabits and is alert to the cues that will signal this difference, full-scale inquiry at this stage is not necessary.

The second issue here is sourcing and supervising commissioned research. Managers who do not have in-house research resources will have to place contracts with university research groups and commercial research houses. In the qualitative area, there are a great many individuals practicing qualitative research who began with bad training and who have devoted their careers to tightening the limitations this training has put on their powers of observation. (I, for one, have seen tens of thousands of dollars spent on commercial and university-based qualitative research so badly conducted that the results were either useless or dangerously misleading.) As a result, research should never be commissioned from a third-party without an insider's advice and/or very careful shopping. This is emphatically not to say that good researchers cannot be found. It is to say that advice must be sought, and care taken. Caveat emptor!

Once a supplier of research has been found, the manager should feel entirely justified in asking to listen to tapes of interviews, to see interview transcripts, and to monitor the process of analysis as it moves from level to level of generality. This should be done on a spontaneous basis. Some research suppliers are not above stage managing the client's encounters with the research process. All too often clients are wined, dined, and distracted on one side of the glass while their money is being lavished on bad research on the other. The object here to is watch for the points noted in the body of this book and to see that data collection and analysis satisfies the conditions specified in Chapters 3 and 4.

The third issue is that of judging the quality and usefulness of the data received. The manager has the right to ask for analysis that includes verbatim quotes from the interview transcripts, as well as for the records of the successive stages of analysis. The care and precision of the analysis process should have created a "paper trail" and the client is entitled to examine these documents. As Kirk and Miller (1986) have noted, this paper trail is the most assured protector of reliability in qualitative inquiry. The simple measure of usefulness is whether the research allows you to see the world as your respondents see it and allows you to think more formally about the nature of the problem before you.

The fourth area of concern here is integrating results into the larger project. Frequently, a research manager is asked to integrate the results of independent qualitative and quantitative studies. Sometimes this can be done in a useful way. The qualitative data can illuminate what is happening in the quantitative finding, and the quantitative data can demonstrate the scope and distribution of qualitative finding. Just as often, however, the connections are vague and uncertain. Plainly the solution to this problem is to begin the project with an understanding of how quantitative and qualitative data can be used together. Integration here may be a matter of sequencing methods so that a first set of qualitative methods is used to establish categories and test questions, a second set of quantitative methods is used to find relationships, a third set of qualitative methods is used to explore these relationships, and a fourth set of quantitative methods is used to determine their distribution. In other cases, it will be enough only to "triangulate" using the two methods in tandem (Jick, 1979). The ability to mix, match, and orchestrate methods is the research manager's strength and justification. It is perhaps the most important way he or she "adds value" to the research process.

As a closing point, a long-standing problem must be addressed. The manager is frequently called upon to defend his or her data against poachers. Qualitative data, like quantitative data, are very sensitive to how they are framed. The same datum can be used to say many things. Every organization possesses individuals who are skilled and practiced in the art of snapping up bits of qualitative data and using them to make their case. There is no simple defense. Managers can only shepherd results so that the risk is diminished. The tighter the project and the more careful the analysis, the easier is the defense (and the easier it is to embarrass those who come poaching).

Administered Research

Let us now consider the social scientist who serves as the principal investigator on a team of researchers and graduate students. In this case, the researcher may be unable to perform his or her own interviews or fully to perform his or her own analysis and write-up. It is possible to delegate research responsibilities of this kind as long as certain precautions are taken.

The first of these is training. Researchers who are going to collect data should be given a full week of training in addition to a course in qualitative methods. They should be given the opportunity to go through the full cycle of the long interview process and their progress at each stage should be monitored and discussed.

Students who are going to do some of the analysis for a project need still more extensive and detailed training. At the very least, students should have completed a course in which the basics of qualitative methods are discussed, and they should then have two full weeks of training. Students who are going to be used for analysis should also be screened for native talent. It is worth having several pages of qualitative data and a set of general questions at hand as a screening device.

The administered interview follows the same four steps as the conventional long interview process, with several modifications. The first step reviews the academic literature except that in this case the research administrator sends researchers out to collect and perhaps also review the literature. The second step, the cultural review, can also be delegated to a team of researchers. However, the principal investigator should make every effort to participate in this step with his or her research team, which then reviews the categories, assumptions, and patterns that are salient to the topic in question. With the results of the first and second steps, the administrator must then carefully supervise the construction of the questionnaire so that it conforms to the conditions noted in Chapter 3. Questionnaire construction cannot be delegated.

It is here in the third step that the most striking changes in the research process take place. Instead of creating a single questionnaire and undertaking a number of interviews, the administrator may wish to make several passes so that data collection and analysis happens in stages. In the first pass, researchers take out a questionnaire to complete a small number of interviews, and then return to transcribe important passages, identify key words, and examine the data for their formal properties. These data are then reviewed by the administrator, who may then wish to formulate a second set of questions and send his or her researchers back out into the field to ask a more precise or different set of questions. This process can be continued until the administrator is persuaded that the key matters have been uncovered and that there is sufficient data for thorough analysis.

The fourth step can also be delegated to researchers who do the initial passes, identifying categories and assumptions and the context of the interview in which they occur. These are then turned over to the administrator for examination, and he or she in turn may ask the researchers to go back to the analysis process with a more particular set of objectives.

The virtue of this managed version of the long interview is that it allows the administrator to intervene at crucial moments of the research process and ensure that the standards and objectives of the long interview are being accomplished. It spares the administrator the responsibility of having to create and manage the large amounts of time and attention that must be given to the research process without alienating him or her from its essential aspects.

The research manager may also wish to use a team approach to qualitative inquiry. A group of researchers can undertake each of the four steps of the long interview process collectively. This team approach can be particularly valuable in the second step. Using "brain-storming" sessions, members of the research team try to provoke one another to break through the received assumptions that conceal the cultural logic of the topic under study. Before beginning group sessions, however, it is important to give each individual the opportunity to formulate an independent cultural review in order to avoid the consensus effect of group interaction. The multiplier effect of group interaction here serves as a substitute for long and careful reflection by a single individual. This process will help broaden and refine topic identification, as well as sharpen the acquaintance and maximize the distance the investigator will eventually bring to bear on the data.

The third step of the long interview can also be undertaken on a collective basis. The interview itself can be conducted with a single interviewer and two or three additional observers. The interview should be taped, but it should also be broadcast (as it is in the focus group) to a soundproof location in which observers can work as the interview is taking place. Their responsibility is to identify and analyze key terms and assumptions as these emerge. Two of these observers should be identifying key passages, noting their place on the tape, and jotting a summary of what was said. They should work in tandem so that while one is noting an important passage, the other can be listening for new passages. A third observer should be listening to the tape from a more general perspective in an attempt to build up an overall picture of the interview and its continuities and themes. On the completion of the interview, the interviewer and observers should confer. They must consult their notes and one another so that key passages can be identified and then transcribed.

Analysis should proceed by the same graduated stages described in Chapter 3. For the opening stages of research, members of the team should work on their own. They should return to their understanding of the literature and the culture review, and begin the process of identifying key terms and assumptions. These should be allowed to generate comments and the comments then generate comments of their own. At this point, the team reassembles to compare notes. It is worthwhile, borrowing a page from the Delphi process of expert interviewing (Linstone and Turoff, 1975), to ask each team member to write his or her conclusions out before the group begins its deliberations. After deliberations are complete, these conclusions should be recited and dealt with individually. This technique prevents the consensus effect of committee work from driving certain interpretive possibilities from consideration. It forces the group to make a conscious and deliberate decision on its options.

In sum, the four-step method of inquiry can take the form of commissioned or administered research. In both of these instances, the method is managed by a single individual who enlists or directs a team of researchers. Naturally, there is a potential problem here. The role of managing the four-step method can take the investigator away from the interview process and away from the fine ethnographic detail of the respondent's testimony. The manager must labor to ensure that he or she is not so removed from the interview process that it is no longer possible to see and experience the world as the respondent does. Only vigilance can prevent this state of methodological alienation from taking place.

7. CONCLUSION

The long qualitative interview has many special virtues. It gives the investigator an agile instrument with which to capture how the respondent sees and experiences the world. It does so in such a way that neither the investigator nor the respondent must make extraordinary sacrifices in time or privacy.

But the four-step method of inquiry is also designed to take account of several additional issues that confront the practice of qualitative methods in modern North America. It is designed to draw upon other social scientific research methods and other versions of qualitative inquiry. It is hoped that this will contribute to stronger links between donor disciplines and qualitative practice, and better cooperation between the traditions of qualitative practice. The four-part method is also designed to allow investigators to exploit their familiarity with their own culture so that they may design better questions, listen more skillfully, and analyze data with greater sensitivity. But it also seeks to help them transcend this familiarity so that it does not blunt their critical skills. Third, the long interview is designed to give the investigator a means of collecting and treating qualitative data so that it may be both abundant and manageable. It is designed to capture the famous "richness" of qualitative data without setting the investigator adrift on a featureless sea. Finally, the method is designed to fashion a relationship between investigator and respondent that honors what each party should and should not give to the other.

The major objective of the method is to help the investigator accomplish ethnographic objectives in the face of the considerable difficulties and constraints that pertain in modern North America. It is hoped that this four-step method of inquiry will create a research instrument of this character, and that this treatment of it will contribute to the codification of qualitative methods that Barton and Lazarsfeld (1955) called for some 30 years ago but that is only now underway.

APPENDIX A
PRELIMINARY QUESTIONS
FOR QUALITATIVE RESEARCH PROJECT

Today's Date:
Place:
Time:
Interviewer's Name:

Subject's Name:
Birth (Maiden) Name:
Sex:
Birth Date:
Age:
Birth Place:

Residence Pattern:

born in

	till		big, medium, little, village, rural
	till		big, medium, little, village, rural
	till		big, medium, little, village, rural
	till		big, medium, little, village, rural

Special Comment: (e.g., military family, moved every 5 years)

Birth Order: 1st ____ 2nd ____ 3rd ____ 4th ____ 5th

Brothers:
first name _____ present age ____ now lives in _____
first name _____ present age ____ now lives in _____
first name _____ present age ____ now lives in _____
first name _____ present age ____ now lives in _____

Sisters:
first name _____ present age ____ now lives in _____
first name _____ present age ____ now lives in _____
first name _____ present age ____ now lives in _____
first name _____ present age ____ now lives in _____

67

Parents:
mother age _____ died in what year _____ your age then _____
father age _____ died in what year _____ your age then _____

Marital Status: divorced ____ you were how old: ____
mother remarried when you were ____
father remarried when you were ____
lived with mother between ages ____ and ____
lived with father between ages ____ and ____

Special Comments:

Place of birth of mother: _____ stepmother _____
Place of birth of father: _____ stepfather _____

Ethnic background of mother: _____ stepmother _____
Ethnic background of father: _____ stepfather _____

Occupation of mother: _____ stepmother _____
Occupation of father: _____ stepfather _____

Respondent's Education:

highest level:
emphasis/specialty (if any):

Occupation:

Marital Status and History:

married what year: ____
divorced what year: ____
remarried what year: ____
remarried what year: ____

Children:
(ages and gender)

name: _____ age: ____ gender: ____ now living: ____
name: _____ age: ____ gender: ____ now living: ____
name: _____ age: ____ gender: ____ now living: ____
name: _____ age: ____ gender: ____ now living: ____
name: _____ age: ____ gender: ____ now living: ____

Religion:

how religious: strong moderate inactive indifferent

how often worships: daily, weekly, monthly, several times a year, yearly, once
every several years

APPENDIX B
STANDARD ETHICS PROTOCOL

(to be read by interviewer before the beginning of the interview. One copy of this form should be left with the respondent, and one copy should be signed by the respondent and kept by the interviewer)

Hi, my name is _____. I am a researcher/research assistant on a project entitled:

_____

This project is being sponsored by the Department of _____ at the University of _____.

I am (Professor x is) the principal investigator of this project and I (he/she) may be contacted at this phone number _____ should you have any questions.

Thank you for your willingness to participate in this research project. Your participation is very much appreciated. Just before we start the interview, I would like to reassure you that as a participant in this project you have several very definite rights.

First, your participation in this interview is entirely voluntary.

You are free to refuse to answer any question at any time.

You are free to withdraw from the interview at any time.

This interview will be kept strictly confidential and will be available only to members of the research team.

Excerpts of this interview may be made part of the final research report, but under no circumstances will your name or identifying characteristics be included in this report.

I would be grateful if you would sign this form to show that I have read you its contents.

_____ (signed)
_____ (printed)
_____ (dated)

Please send me a report on the results of this research project. (circle one)

YES   NO

address for those requesting research report

_____
_____
_____
_____

(Interviewer: keep signed copy; leave unsigned copy with respondent)

APPENDIX C
BUDGET ITEMS AND CALCULATIONS

Qualitative researchers who are planning a qualitative project and/or applying for research funding may find the following budget considerations useful.
EQUIPMENT

Tape recorders **characteristics**: high quality cassette, separate microphone (not built-in), external power source (not batteries), audible tape-finished signal, visible power-on light, reliable tape counter, long extension cord. **number**: one per interviewer. **note**: should be calibrated periodically (tape recorders can lose their calibration and create tapes that cannot be read on the transcriber); consider back-up tape-recorder.

Transcribing machine **characteristics**: high quality, foot pedal for tape movement, variable tape speed control, head phones. **number**: potential bottleneck for projects on tight schedule; considering getting more than one. **note**: should be calibrated periodically

Tape **characteristics**: high quality cassettes, not over 30 minutes per side. **note**: establish detailed labelling system for tape cassette and tape cassette container, include date, time, interviewer's name, interviewee's name, and sequence number

Software **characteristics**: (1) sophisticated word processor (e.g., Microsoft Word, Word Perfect). **number**: one per transcriber, one per analyst (2) sophisticated index and search programs (e.g., ZyIndex, AskSam). **number**: one per analyst. **note**: considered budgeting for costs of software up-grades (e.g., 10% of software cost)

Hardware **characteristics**: (1) personal computer (MS-DOS or OS/2) **characteristics**: fast chip; sufficient memory to run software; screen must have excellent text resolution. **number**: one per transcriber; one per analyst. **note**: watch for bottle necks here; avoid relying on existing machines that cannot be made routinely available for the long periods of transcription and analysis; project-dedicated machine(s) desirable (2) hard (fixed) disk **characteristics**: fast access time, sufficient memory to accommodate all transcribed data. **number**: for analysts only. **note**: project-dedicated hard disk(s) desirable

Floppy disks **characteristics**: appropriate to computer **number**: sufficient to transport and archive transcribed data

Filing cabinets **characteristics**: lockable, sufficient space to contain tapes, back-up diskettes, printed versions of transcription, equipment, interview records. **note**: claim to confidentiality depends on locked storage

Maintenance **characteristics:** budgets should include money for the maintenance of equipment (e.g., 10% of equipment costs).

Sample budget (labor only for project with 8 respondents)
contact
1 hour per respondent $\times$ 8 respondents = 8 contact hours
training
40 hours $\times$ 1 interviewer = 40 hours
80 hours $\times$ 1 analyst = 80 hours
interviews
3 hours per respondent $\times$ 8 respondents = 24 interview hours
transport
1 hour per respondent $\times$ 8 respondents = 8 transport hours
transcription
4 hrs transcription $\times$ 24 interview hrs = 96 transcription hrs
analysis
5 hrs analysis $\times$ 24 interview hrs = 120 analysis hours
write-up
5 hours write-up $\times$ 24 interview hrs = 120 write-up hours
project management
half day for duration of project (4 $\times$ 60d) = 240 mgmt hours
Total: 736 hours

APPENDIX D

This appendix suggests topics that may prove useful for students learning qualitative methods.

Topics:

I have listed several possible topics under the headings "events, activities and processes," "conditions," and "institutions." Each of these categories encourages a slightly different set of objectives and strategies. These are briefly noted.

EVENTS, ACTIVITIES and PROCESSES:

buying a home
watching tv
making the evening meal
getting ready for a special occasion
Christmas
patterns of belonging at a home for the elderly
watching soap operas
reading a magazine
buying a car
gardening
planning the perfect home
walking the dog

planning the perfect holiday
developing a new product
managing a small business
creating a marketing campaign
eating at McDonald's

Objectives and strategies:

The objective in investigating a topic in this category is to "get under" the commonplace view of the activity and see how the individual really sees and experiences it.

One way to set about systematically gathering information to do this is to think about the event, activity, or process as a dramatic production. You must determine what the important roles are, who will occupy these roles, how well the roles are enacted, who the director and prompter of the proceedings is, what the stage is, how the action is organized and scheduled, who the audience is, who the critics are, what is accomplished for actors and audiences when the production goes well, what happens, on the other hand, when the production goes badly, what kind of things can go wrong, how they will be set right, and so on.

Again, the object is to get past the formal and ordinary description of the event into hidden social and cultural realities. For instance, it would be easy enough to go out and collect a set of statements about what Christmas is. Respondents are willing to trot out a set of conventional descriptions: Christmas is a time to celebrate a religious occasion, get together with family, exchange gifts, and look back on the year. But this would not tell us anything new about Christmas and it certainly would not justify the time, difficulty, and expense of qualitative investigation.

But the careful investigator through patient questioning and intelligent listening can learn much more. What he or she wants to do is to determine some of the following questions: what activities make up Christmas, when does each of them start, who undertakes them, what part does gender play here; what does Christmas decoration do to the character of the home, how do people decide what to buy for one another; what are the consequences of a good gift and a bad one; how do families plan for their time together; what diplomatic preparations are made to make sure that people get along and "Grandpa Henry and Uncle Rubert don't get at one another this year"; how the nature of family interaction changes in the Christmas season; how does participating in the ritual and gift exchange of Christmas have short-term and long term consequences for how the family defines itself and gets along; what family activities are particular to the Christmas season; what difference will it make to the nature of family interaction if the activity is (1) watching a football game, (2) going for a walk in the country, (3) going to a movie; sometimes Christmas means that men spend more time around the house than usual, how do they respond; what do children learn about their families and their societies at Christmas; what special role do women play in organizing Christmas and family life at Christmas?

It is worth pointing out here that most of these questions cannot be asked directly. They can be answered only by asking other questions, and piecing answers together. It is also worth pointing out that there is astonishingly little social scientific literature on the topic of Christmas, and that those who choose this topic for qualitative research will have the satisfaction and challenge of travelling relatively uncharted ground.

CONDITIONS:

being elderly
being upper middle class
being poor
being a pet owner
being handicapped
being an artist
being a wrestling fan
being a university administrator
being a public attorney
being gay
being a preppie
being a jock
being a single parent
being illiterate
being a comedian
being rich
being a feminist
being a conservative
being a college freshman
being a cocktail waitress
being a college senior

Objectives and strategies:

The object here is to see whether you can "climb into the head" of one of these people and see the world as they do. What are the important categories into which the world is organized, how do these categories fit together, on what assumptions do they rest and so on. One useful way of accomplishing this is by setting up a contrast between two groups. You might contrast how the university administrator sees the university with how a freshman sees it. Compare the world view of a public defender and a rich attorney.

INSTITUTIONS:

advertising
the art world

banking system
Hollywood
insurance system
legislative process
scientific research community
museums
nature
political system
medical doctors
post office
senate
supreme court
the European common market
the family
the founding fathers
the social security system
the United Nations
universities
World War II
the Korean war

Objectives and strategies:

The object here is to determine how people "really" see these institutions. It is easy for us to assume that people share a single understanding of what World War II was, how the senate works, or who the founding fathers were and what they did. In fact, it is so easy for us to assume that there is agreement here that we rarely check to see if this is indeed the case. On those few occasions that social scientists do check to with the "person in the street" the results are sometimes astonishing. Frequently people prove to have their own quite peculiar ideas about how the world is constituted.

The great advantage of qualitative methods is that it gives the investigator a chance to hear these ideas and capture them in all of their unexpected novelty. The object then is to get respondents to describe these institutions, noting their components parts, the processes by which they work, what their objectives are, how they really work, what they accomplish for the individual, what they accomplish for society.

This, too, is uncharted ground. What you will be hearing in the investigation of some of these topics is totally unexplored material. It is also very important research. It is extraordinarily useful for the institutions in question to understand how they are viewed by their public and the misconceptions at work there.

NOTES

1. For examples of this rich tradition in sociology, see Banks (1957), Becker (1954, 1956, 1958), Becker and Geer (1957, 1958), Benney and Hughes (1956), Cannell and Axelrod (1956), Caplow (1956), Gorden (1956), Merton et al. (1956), Merton and Kendall (1946), Schwartz and Schwartz (1955), Strauss and Schatzman (1955), Trow (1957), Vidich (1955), Vidich and Shapiro (1955), Von Hoffman and Cassidy (1956), Wax (1952), Wax and Shapiro (1956), and Whyte (1955, 1957, 1960).

2. Some of the recent developments in sociology include Emerson (1983), Howe (1985), Lofland (1976), Lofland and Lofland (1984), O'Neill (1985), Psathas (1973), Reinharz (1979), Schwartz and Jacobs (1979), Shaffir et al. (1980), Silverman (1985), and Truzzi (1974).

3. These psychologists include Gergen and Gergen (1986), Ginsburg (1979), Giorgi (1970, 1985), Harre and Secord (1972), Kruger (1979), Reasons and Rowan (1981), and Willems and Rausch (1969).

4. For contributors to this development in anthropology, see Agar (1980, 1983a, 1983b), Clifford and Marcus (1986), Ellen (1984), Epstein (1967), Foster et al. (1979), Freilich (1970), Hammersley and Atkinson (1983), Lawless et al. (1983), McDermott et al. (1978), Messerschmidt (1981), Rabinow (1977), Rabinow and Sullivan (1979), Salamone (1977), Spradley (1979), Srinivas et al. (1979), Werner and Schoepfle (1987), and Whittaker (1985).

5. Contributors to the field of administrative studies include Cook and Reichardt (1979), Goetz and LeCompte (1984), Borman et al. (1986), Lincoln and Guba (1985), Miles (1979), Miles and Huberman (1984), Morgan (1983), Morgan and Smircich (1980), Patton (1980), Rist (1977), Van Maanen (1982, 1983), Van Maanen et al. (1982), and Wilson (1977).

6. For literature on the focus group, see ARF (1985), Bartos (1986), Bellenger et al. (1976), Calder (1977), Fern (1982), Goldman (1962), Higginbotham and Cox (1979), (especially) Moran (1986), Overholser (1986), Sampson (1972a), Snell (1987), and Wells (1986).

7. New methods in consumer behavior research are discussed in Barnett (1985), Belk (1986, 1987), Berent (1966), Durgee (1986a, 1986b), Hirschman (1985), Hirschman and Holbrook (1986), Holbrook (1987a, 1987b), May (1978), Sherry (1987), and Wallendorf (1987).

8. For more on sociolinguistics, see Albert and Kessler (1978), Bauman and Sherzer (1974), Briggs (1986), Churchill (1973), Goffman (1976), Gumperz and Hymes (1972), Sacks et al. (1974), Schegloff and Sacks (1973), and Schiffrin (1977).

9. The qualitative/quantitative debate is taken up in Anderson (1986), Borman et al. (1986), Brown and Sime (1982), Bryman (1984), Cronbach (1975), Deshpande (1983), Harre (1981), Morgan and Smircich (1980), Ratcliffe (1983), and Smith and Heshusius (1986).

10. For most purposes, the best way of striking this balance in men's clothing is a sweater, sports jacket, and tie ensemble so widely adopted by professional counselors. Female colleagues tell me the same effect can be achieved by a suit with a full, pleated skirt, a soft or tailored blouse open at the throat, low-heeled shoes, with restrained makeup and jewelry.

11. For more on the method of participant observation, see Agar (1983a, 1986), Becker (1956, 1958), Becker and Geer (1957), Bogdan and Taylor (1975), Ellen (1984), Foster et al. (1979), Halle (1984), Hammersley and Atkinson (1983), Kluckhohn (1940), Lerner (1956), McCall and Simon (1969), Miller (1952), Olesen and Whittaker (1967), Reinharz (1979), Schwartz and Becker (1971), Schwartz and Schwartz (1955), Trow (1957), Vidich and Shapiro (1955), Vidich (1955), and Whyte (1955, 1984).

12. For more on focus groups, see the references in note 6 above.

13. Repertory grid analysis is designed to allow for the statistical treatment of categories and scales created by the respondent. For more on this method, see Chambers (1985), Chambers and Grice (1986), Collett (1979), Durgee (1986a), MacFarlane-Smith (1972), and Sampson (1972b.

14. For more on life histories, see Bennis (1968), Bromley (1986), Campbell (1975), Cavan et al. (1930), Denzin (1978a), Dollard (1935), Frank (1979), Langness (1965), Little (1980), Tagg (1985), Van Velsen (1967), and Watson and Watson-Franke (1985).

15. For more on case studies, see Bennis (1968), Bonoma (1985), Bromley (1986), Campbell (1975), Leenders and Erskine (1973), McClintock et al. (1979), and Stake (1978).

16. Protocols are created when respondents describe their interior states and decision-making processes as they perform certain activities. For more on this method, see Bettman (1979) and Ericsson and Simon (1980).

17. For more on the diary method, see Atkinson (1985), Norris (1987), and Zimmerman and Wieder (1977).

18. The following authors have addressed this issue: Brown and Sime (1982), Campbell and Fiske (1959), Canter et al. (1985), Cavan et al. (1930), Jick (1979), McClintock et al. (1979), Myers (1977), Rist (1977), Sieber (1973), Sproull and Sproull (1982), Tagg (1985), Trend (1979), Vidich and Shapiro (1955).

19. The term "culture categories" is defined, discussed, and illustrated in McCracken (1988b).

20. This is, incidentally, a factor to be kept in mind when researchers are judging the amount of time that will be needed to accomplish a number of interviews. In my own experience, one interview per day is the best rule of thumb. I have tried two interviews a day, but I found that fatigue set in after three successive days.

21. This program, and others like it, are reviewed in Badgett (1987). Other uses of computer technology in the treatment of qualitative data are reviewed in Bernard and Evans (1983), Chambers and Grice (1986), Cohen (1985), Collett (1979), Conrad and Reinharz (1984), Mostyn (1985), Podolefsky and McCarty (1983), Richards and Richards (1987), and Sproull and Sproull (1982).

22. This list is culled from Bunge's "The Weight of Simplicity in the Construction and Assaying of Scientific Theories." It is worth pointing out that Bunge's original scheme of 20 "assaying criteria" was designed for the assessment of natural scientific theory, not social scientific explanation. It is also worth noting that seven conditions suggested here are intended as a rough and ready categorical scheme that makes up in usefulness what it lacks in philosophical rigor.

23. Social scientists already familiar with the qualitative write-up process may wish to skip this chapter.

24. Readers are asked to remember that the write-up model proposed here is simply one way of approaching the problem. It is also worth pointing out that experimentation is now going on in this area (Marcus and Fischer, 1986; Van Maanen, 1988). The following guidelines are offered more in the spirit of suggestion than prescription.

REFERENCES

ABLON, J. (1977) "Field method in working with middle class Americans: new issues of values, personality, and reciprocity." Human Organization 36 (1): 69-72.

ALBERT, S. and S. KESSLER (1978) "Ending social encounters." J. of Experimental Social Psychology 14 (6): 541-553.

AGAR, M. H. (1980) The Professional Stranger: An Informal Introduction to Ethnography. New York: Academic Press.

AGAR, M. H. (1983a) "Ethnographic evidence." Urban Life 12 (1): 32-48.

AGAR, M. H. (1983b) "Inference and schema: an ethnographic view." Human Studies 6: 53-66.

AGAR, M. H. (1986) Independents Declared: The Dilemmas of Independent Trucking. Washington, DC: Smithsonian Institution Press.

ANDERSON, P. (1986) "On method in consumer research: a critical relativist perspective." J. of Consumer Research 13 (2): 155-173.

ARF (Advertising Research Foundation) (1985) Focus Groups: Issues and Approaches. New York: Advertising Research Foundation.

ATKINSON, D. (1985) "The use of participant observation and respondent diaries in a study of ordinary living." British J. of Mental Subnormality 31/1 (60): 33-39.

BADGETT, T. (1987) "Searching through files with database software." PC Magazine 6 (18 October): 175-190.

BANKS, J. A. (1957) "The group discussion as an interview technique." Soc. Rev. 5 (1): 75-84.

BARNETT, S. (1985) "Everyday life ethnography: case studies of dishwashing and diapering," pp. 31-42 in C. Clark (ed.) On Beyond Interviewing: Observational Studies of Consumer Behavior. Chicago, IL: Conference Proceedings, October 10.

BARTON, A. H. and P. F. LAZARSFELD (1955) "Some functions of qualitative analysis in social research." Frankfurter Beitrage Zur Soziologie Band 1: 321-361.

BARTOS, R. (1986) "Qualitative research: what it is and where it came from." J. of Advertising Research 26 (3).

BAUMAN, R. and J. SHERZER (eds.) (1974) Explorations in the Ethnography of Speaking. New York: Cambridge Univ. Press.

BECKER, H. S. (1954) "Field notes and techniques: a note on interviewing tactics." Human Organization 12 (4): 31-32.

BECKER, H. S. (1956) "Interviewing medical students." Amer. J. of Sociology 62 (2): 199-201.

BECKER, H. S. (1958) "Problems of inference and proof in participant observation." Amer. Soc. Rev. 23 (6): 652-660.

BECKER, H. S. and B. GEER (1957) "Participant observation and interviewing: a comparison." Human Organization 16 (3): 28-32.

BECKER, H. S. and B. GEER (1958) "Participant observation and interviewing: a rejoinder." Human Organization 17 (2): 39-40.

BELK, R. W. (1986) "Art versus science as ways of generating knowledge about materialism," pp. 3-36 in D. Brinberg and R. J. Lutz (eds.) Perspectives on Methodology in Consumer Research. New York: Springer-Verlag.

BELK, R. W. (1987) "The role of the odyssey in consumer behavior and in consumer research," pp. 357-361 in M. Wallendorf and P. Anderson (eds.) Advances in Consumer Research. Provo, UT: Association for Consumer Research.

BELLENGER, D., K. L. BERNHARDT, and J. L. GOLDSTUCKER (1976) Qualitative Research in Marketing. Chicago: American Marketing Association.

BENNEY, M. and E. C. HUGHES (1956) "Of sociology and the interview: editorial preface." Amer. J. of Sociology 62 (September): 137-142.

BENNIS, W. G. (1968) "The case study." J. of Applied Behavioral Science 4 (2): 227-231.

BERENT, P. H. (1966) "The technique of the depth interview." J. of Advertising Research 6 (2): 32-39.

BERNARD, H. R. and M. J. EVANS (1983) "New microcomputer techniques for anthropologists." Human Organization 42 (2): 182-185.

BERREMAN, G. D. (1966) "Anemic and emetic analyses in social anthropology." Amer. Anthropologist 68 (2): 346-354.

BETTMAN, J. R. (1979) An Information Processing Theory of Consumer Choice. Reading, MA: Addison-Wesley.

BOGDAN, R. and S. J. TAYLOR (1975) Introduction of Qualitative Research Methods: A Phenomenological Approach to the Social Sciences. New York: John Wiley.

BONOMA, T. (1985) "Case research in marketing: opportunities, problems and a process." J. of Marketing Research 22 (May): 199-208.

BORMAN, K. M., M. D. LECOMPTE, and J. P. GOETZ (1986) "Ethnographic and qualitative research design and why it doesn't work." Amer. Behavioral Scientist 30 (1): 42-57.

BRENNER, M. (1985) "Intensive Interviewing," pp. 147-162 in M. Brenner, J. Brown, and D. Canter (eds.) The Research Interview: Uses and Approaches. London: Academic Press.

BRIGGS, C. L. (1986) Learning How to Ask: A Sociolinguistic Appraisal of the Role of the Interview in Social Science Research. New York: Cambridge Univ. Press.

BROMLEY, D. (1986) The Case Study Method in Psychology and Related Disciplines. New York: John Wiley.

BROWN, J. M. and J. D. SIME (1982) "Multidimensional scaling analysis of qualitative data," pp. 71-90 in E. Shepherd and J. P. Watson (eds.) Personal Meanings: The First Guy's Hospital Symposium on the Individual Frame of Reference. New York: John Wiley.

BRYMAN, A. (1984) "The debate about quantitative and qualitative research." British J. of Sociology 35 (1): 75-92.

BUNGE, M. (1961) "The weight of simplicity in the construction and assaying of scientific theories." Philosophy of Sci. 28 (2): 120-149.

CALDER, B. (1977) "Focus groups and the nature of qualitative marketing research." J. of Marketing Research 14 (August): 353-364.

CAMPBELL, D. T. (1955) "The informant in qualitative research." Amer. J. of Sociology 60 (4): 339-342.

CAMPBELL, D. T. (1975) "'Degrees of freedom' and the case study." Comparative Pol. Studies 8: 178-193.

CAMPBELL, D. T. and D. W. FISKE (1959) "Convergent and discriminant validation by the multitrait-multimethod matrix." Psych. Bull. 56: 81-105.

CANNELL, C. F. and M. AXELROD (1956) "The respondent reports on the interview." Amer. J. of Sociology 62 (2): 177-181.

CANNELL, C. F., F. J. FOWLER, Jr., and K. H. MARQUIS (1968) The Influence of Interviewer and Respondent Psychological and Behavioral Variables on the Reporting in Household Interviews, Public Health Service, Series 2, Number 26, 1-65. Washington, DC: Department of Health, Education, and Welfare, National Center for Health Statistics.

CANNELL, C. F., L. OKSENBERG, and J. M. CONVERSE (eds.) (1979) Experiments in Interviewing Techniques: Field Experiments in Health Reporting, 1971-1977. Research Report Series. Ann Arbor: University of Michigan, Institute for Social Research.

CANTER, D., J. BROWN, and L. GROAT (1985) "A multiple sorting procedure for studying conceptual systems," pp. 79-114 in M. Brenner, J. Brown, and D. Canter (eds.) The Research Interview: Uses and Approaches. London: Academic Press.

CAPLOW, T. (1956) "The dynamics of information interviewing." Amer. J. of Sociology 62 (2): 165-171.

CASSELL, J. (1977) "The relationship of observer to observed in peer group research." Human Organization 36 (4): 412-416.

CAVAN, R., P. M. HAUSER, and S. A. STOUFFER (1930) "Note on the statistical treatment of life history material." Social Forces 9: 200-203.

CHAMBERS, W. V. (1985) "A repertory grid measure of mandalas." Psych. Reports 57: 923-928.

CHAMBERS, W. V. and J. W. GRICE (1986) "Circumgrids: a repertory grid package for personal computers." Behavior Research Methods, Instruments, and Computers 18 (5): 468.

CHOCK, P. P. (1986) "Irony and ethnography: on cultural analysis of one's own culture." Anthro. Q. 59 (2): 87-96.

CHURCHILL, L. (1973) Questioning Strategies in Sociolinguistics. Rowley, MA: Newbury House.

CLIFFORD, J. and G. E. MARCUS (eds.) (1986) Writing Culture: The Poetics and Politics of Ethnography. Berkeley: Univ. of California Press.

COHEN, R. J. (1985) "Computer-enhanced qualitative research." J. of Advertising Research 25 (3): 48-52.

COLLETT, P. (1979) "The repertory grid in psychological research," pp. 225-252 in G. P. Ginsburg (ed.) Emerging Strategies in Social Psychological Research. New York: John Wiley.

CONRAD, P. and S. REINHARZ (eds.) (1984) "Computers and qualitative data." Qualitative Sociology 7 (1-2): 1-194.

COOK, T. D. and C. S. REICHARDT (eds.) (1979) Qualitative and Quantitative Methods in Evaluation Research. Beverly Hills, CA: Sage.

CRONBACH, L. (1975) "Beyond the two disciplines of scientific psychology." Amer. Psychologist 30: 116-127.

DENZIN, N. K. (1978a) "The comparative life history method," pp. 214-255 in N. K. Denzin, The Research Act. New York: McGraw-Hill.

DENZIN, N. K. (1978b) "The sociological interview," pp. 112-134 in N. K. Denzin, The Research Act. New York: McGraw-Hill.

DESHPANDE, R. (1983) "Paradigms lost: on theory and method in research in marketing." J. of Marketing 47 (Fall): 101-110.

DOHRENWEND, B. S. and S. A. RICHARDSON (1956) "Analysis of the interviewer's behavior." Human Organization 15 (2): 29-32.

DOLLARD, J. (1935) Criteria for the Life History. New Haven: Yale Univ. Press.

DOUGLAS, J. D. (1976) Investigative Social Research. Beverly Hills, CA: Sage.

DUBOIS, C. (1937) "Some psychological objectives and techniques in ethnology." J. of Social Psychology 3: 285-301.

DURGEE, J. F. (1986a) "Depth-interviewing techniques for creative advertising." J. of Advertising Research 25 (6): 29-37.

DURGEE, J. F. (1986b) "Richer findings from qualitative research." J. of Advertising Research 26 (4): 36-44.

ELDEN, M. (1981) "Sharing the research work: participative research and its role demands," pp. 253-266 in P. Reasons and J. Rowan (eds.) Human Inquiry: A Sourcebook of New Paradigm Research. Chichester: John Wiley.

ELLEN, R. F. (ed.) (1984) "Ethnographic research: a guide to general conduct." London: Academic Press.

EMERSON, R. M. (ed.) (1983) Contemporary Field Research. Boston: Little, Brown.

EMERSON, R. M. (1987) "Four ways to improve the craft of fieldwork." J. of Contemporary Ethnography 16 (1): 69-89.

EPSTEIN, A. L. (ed.) (1967) The Craft of Social Anthropology. London: Tavistock.

ERICSSON, K. A. and H. A. SIMON (1980) "Verbal reports as data." Psych. Rev. 87 (3): 215-251.

EVANS-PRITCHARD, E. E. (1961) "Social anthropology: past and present," pp. 13-28 in E. E. Evans-Pritchard, Essays in Social Anthropology. London: Faber & Faber.

FALCIGLIA, G., D. WAHLBRINK, and D. SUSZKIW (1985) "Factors of change in elderly eating-related behaviors: an anthropological perspective." J. of Nutrition for the Elderly 5 (1): 67-77.

FERN, E. F. (1982) "The use of focus groups for idea generation: the effects of group size, acquaintanceship and moderator on response quantity and quality." J. of Marketing Research 19 (February): 1-13.

FOSTER, G. M., T. SCUDDER, E. COLSON, and R. V. KEMPER (eds.) (1979) Long-Term Field Research in Social Anthropology. New York: Academic Press.

FRANK, G. (1979) "Finding the common denominator: a phenomenological critique of life history." Ethos 7: 68-94.

FREILICH, M. (ed.) (1970) Marginal Natives At Work: Anthropologists in the Field. New York: Harper & Row.

GEERTZ, C. (1976) "From the native's point of view: on the nature of anthropological understanding," pp. 221-237 in K. Basso and H. A. Selby (eds.) Meaning in Anthropology. Albuquerque, NM: Univ. of New Mexico Press.

GEERTZ, C. (1979) "Deep play: notes on the Balinese cockfight," pp. 181-233 in P. Rabinow and W. M. Sullivan (eds.) Interpretive Social Science: A Reader. Berkeley: Univ. of California Press.

GERGEN, K. J. and M. GERGEN (1986) "Narrative form and the construction of psychological science," pp. 22-44 in T. R. Sarbin (ed.) Narrative Psychology. New York: Praeger.

GINSBURG, G. P. (ed.) (1979) Emerging Strategies in Social Psychological Research. New York: John Wiley.

GIORGI, A. (1970) Psychology as a Human Science: A Phenomenologically Based Approach. New York: Harper & Row.

GIORGI, A. (ed.) (1985) Phenomenology and Psychological Research. Pittsburgh: Duguesne Univ. Press.

GLASER, B. G. and A. L. STRAUSS (1965) "The discovery of substantive theory: a basic strategy underlying qualitative research." Amer. Behavioral Scientist 8 (6): 5-12.

GLASER, B. G. and A. L. STRAUSS (1968) The Discovery of Grounded Theory: Strategies for Qualitative Research. London: Weidenfeld & Nicolson.

GOETZ, J. P. and M. D. LECOMPTE (1984) Ethnography and Qualitative Design in Educational Research. Orlando, FL: Academic Press.

GOFFMAN, E. (1976) "Replies and responses." Language in Society 5: 257-313.

GOLDMAN, A. E. (1962) "The group depth interview." J. of Marketing 26 (3): 61-68.

GORDEN, R. (1956) "Dimensions of depth interview." Amer. J. of Sociology 62 (2): 158-164.

GREENHOUSE, C. J. (1985) "Anthropology at home: whose home?" Human Organization 44 (3): 261-264.

GROSS, N. and W. S. MASON (1953) "Some methodological problems of eight-hour interviews." Amer. J. of Sociology 59 (3): 197-204.

GUBA, E. S. and Y. S. LINCOLN (1981) Effective Evaluation. San Francisco: Jossey-Bass.

GUMPERZ, J. J. and D. HYMES (eds.) (1972) Directions in Sociolinguistics: The Ethnography of Communication. New York: Holt, Rinehart & Winston.

HALLE, D. (1984) America's Working Man: Work, Home and Politics among Blue-Collar Property Owners. Chicago: Univ. of Chicago Press.

HAMMERSLEY, M. and P. ATKINSON (1983) Ethnography: Principles in Practice. London: Tavistock.

HARRE, R. (1981) "The positivist-empiricist approach and its alternative," pp. 3-17 in P. Reasons and J. Rowan (eds.) Human Inquiry: A Sourcebook of New Paradigm Research. Chichester: John Wiley.

HARRE, R. and P. F. SECORD (1972) The Explanation of Social Behavior. Blackwell: Oxford.

HIGGINBOTHAM, J. B. and K. K. COX (eds.) (1979) Focus Group Interviews: A Reader. Chicago: American Marketing Assn.

HIRSCHMAN, E. C. (1985) "Scientific style and the conduct of consumer research." J. of Consumer Research 12 (2): 225-239.

HIRSCHMAN, E. C. and M. B. HOLBROOK (1986) "Expanding the ontology and methodology of research on the consumption experience," pp. 213-251 in D. Brinberg and R. J. Lutz (eds.) Perspectives on Methodology in Consumer Research. New York: Springer-Verlag.

HOLBROOK, M. B. (1987a) "From the log of a consumer researcher," pp. 365-369 in M. Wallendorf and P. Anderson (ed.) Advances in Consumer Research. Provo, UT: Assn. for Consumer Research.

HOLBROOK, M. B. (1987b) "What is consumer research?" J. of Consumer Research 14 (1): 128-132.

HOWE, C. (1985) "Possibilities for using a qualitative research approach in the sociological study of leisure." J. of Leisure Research 17 (3): 212-224.

JICK, T. D. (1979) "Mixing qualitative and quantitative methods: triangulation in action." Admin. Sci. Q. 24 (4): 602-611.

KIRK, J. and M. L. MILLER (1986) Reliability and Validity in Qualitative Research. Beverly Hills, CA: Sage.

KLUCKHOHN, F. R. (1940) "The participant-observer technique in small communities." Amer. J. of Sociology 46 (3): 331-343.

KRUGER, D. (1979) An Introduction to Phenomenological Psychology. Pittsburgh: Duquesne Univ. Press.

KUHN, T. S. (1962) The Structure of Scientific Revolutions. Chicago: Univ. of Chicago Press.

LANGNESS, L. L. (1965) The Life History in Anthropological Science. New York: Holt, Rinehart & Winston.

LAROSSA, R. and J. H. WOLF (1985) "On qualitative family research." J. of Marriage and the Family 46 (August): 531-541.

LAWLESS, R. et al. (eds.) (1983) Fieldwork: The Human Experience. New York: Gordon & Breach Science.

LAZARSFELD, P. E. (1972a) "The art of asking why: three principles underlying the formulation of questionnaires," pp. 183-202 in P. E. Lazarsfeld, Qualitative Analysis. New York: Allyn & Bacon.

LAZARSFELD, P. E. (1972b) Qualitative Analysis: Historical and Critical Essays. Boston: Allyn & Bacon.

LEENDERS, M. R. and J. ERSKINE (1973) Case Research: The Case Writing Process. London, Ontario: University of Western Ontario, School of Business.

LERNER, D. (1956) "Interviewing Frenchmen." Amer. J. of Sociology 62 (2): 187-194.

LEZNOFF, M. (1956) "Interviewing homosexuals." Amer. J. of Sociology 62 (2): 202-204.

LINCOLN, Y. S. and E. G. GUBA (1985) Naturalistic Inquiry. Beverly Hills, CA: Sage.

LINSTONE, H. A. and M. TUROFF (eds.) (1975) The Delphi Method: Techniques and Applications. Reading, MA: Addison-Wesley.

LITTLE, K. (1980) "Explanation and individual lives: a reconsideration of life writing in anthropology." Dialectical Anthropology 5: 215-226.

LOFLAND, J. (1976) Doing Social Life: The Qualitative Study of Social Life. New York: John Wiley.

LOFLAND, J. and L. H. LOFLAND (1984) Analyzing Social Settings: A Guide to Qualitative Observation and Analysis. Belmont, CA: Wadsworth.

MacFARLANE-SMITH, J. (1972) Interviewing in Market and Social Research. London: Routledge & Kegan Paul.

MARCUS, G. E. and M.M.J. FISCHER (1986) Anthropology as Cultural Critique: An Experimental Moment in the Human Sciences. Chicago: Univ. of Chicago Press.

MAY, J. P. (1978) "Qualitative advertising research: a review of the role of the researcher." J. of the Market Research Society 20 (4).

McCALL, G. J. and J. L. SIMON (eds.) (1969) Issues in Participant Observation: A Text and Reader. Reading, MA: Addison-Wesley.

McCLINTOCK, C., D. BRANNON, and S. MAYNARD-MOODY (1979) "Applying the logic of sample surveys to qualitative case studies: the case cluster method." Admin. Sci. Q. 24 (December): 612-629.

McCRACKEN, G. (1986) "*Upstairs/Downstairs*: the Canadian production. The cultural and communicative properties of one Canadian home," pp. 68-71 in J. W. Carswell and D. G. Saile (eds.) Purposes in Built Form and Culture Research: Conference Proceedings. Lawrence: University of Kansas.

McCRACKEN, G. (1987) "Culture and consumption among the elderly: three research objectives in an emerging field." Aging and Society 7 (2): 203-224.

McCRACKEN, G. (1988a) "Lois Roget: curatorial consumer in a modern society," pp. 44-53 in G. McCracken, Culture and Consumption: New Approaches to the Symbolism of Consumer Goods and Activities. Bloomington: Indiana Univ. Press.

McCRACKEN, G. (1988b) "Meaning manufacture and movement in the world of goods," pp. 71-89 in G. McCracken, Culture and Consumption: New Approaches to the Symbolism of Consumer Goods and Activities. Bloomington: Indiana Univ. Press.

McDERMOTT, R. P., K. GOSPODINOFF, and J. ARON (1978) "Criteria for an ethnographically adequate description of concerted activities and their activities." Semiotica 24: 245-275.

MERTON, R. K., M. FISKE, and P. L. KENDALL (1956) The Focused Interview: A Manual of Problems and Procedures. New York: Free Press.

MERTON, R. K. and P. L. KENDALL (1946) "The focused interview." Amer. J. of Sociology 51 (6): 541-557.

MESSERSCHMIDT, D. A. (ed.) (1981) Anthropologists at home in North America. Cambridge: Cambridge Univ. Press.

MILES, M. B. (1979) "Qualitative data as an attractive nuisance: the problem of analysis." Admin. Sci. Q. 24 (December): 590-601.

MILES, M. B. and A. M. HUBERMAN (1984) Qualitative Data Analysis: A Sourcebook of New Methods. Beverly Hills, CA: Sage.

MILLER, S. M. (1952) "The Participant Observer and 'Over-Rapport.'" Amer. Soc. Rev. 17 (February): 97-99.

MORAN, W. T. (1986) "The science of qualitative research." J. of Advertising Research 26 (3): RC 16-RC 19.

MORGAN, G. (ed.) (1983) Beyond Method. Beverly Hills, CA: Sage.

MORGAN, G. and L. SMIRCICH (1980) "The case for qualitative research." Academy of Management Rev. 5 (4): 491-500.

MOSTYN, B. (1985) "The content analysis of qualitative research data: a dynamic approach," pp. 115-145 in M. Brenner, J. Brown, and D. Canter (eds.) The Research Interview: Uses and Approaches. London: Academic Press.

MYERS, V. (1977) "Toward a synthesis of ethnographic and survey methods." Human Organization 36: 244-251.

NASH, D. and R. WINTROB (1972) "The emergence of self-consciousness in ethnography." Current Anthropology 13 (5): 527-542.

NORRIS, J. (1987) "Using diaries in gerontological research." Presented at Symposium on Qualitative Methods, Guelph, Ontario, March 13.

O'NEILL, J. (1985) "Phenomenological sociology." Canadian Rev. of Sociology and Anthropology 22 (5): 748-770.

OLESEN, V. L. and E. WHITTAKER (1967) "Role making in participant observation: processes in the researcher-actor relationship." Human Organization 26: 273-281.

OVERHOLSER, C. (1986) "Quality, quantity, and thinking real hard." J. of Advertising Research 26 (3): RC 7-RC 12.

PALMER, V. M. (1928) Field Studies in Sociology: A Student's Manual. Chicago: Univ. of Chicago Press.

PATTON, M. Q. (1980) Qualitative Evaluation Methods. Beverly Hills, CA: Sage.

PAUL, B. D. (1953) "Interview techniques and field techniques," pp. 430-451 in A. L. Kroeber (ed.) Anthropology Today. Chicago: Univ. of Chicago Press.

PIORE, M. J. (1979) "Qualitative research techniques in economics." Admin. Sci. Q. 24 (December): 560-569.

PODOLEFSKY, A. and C. MCCARTY (1983) "Topical sorting: a technique for computer assisted qualitative data analysis." Amer. Anthropologist 85: 886-889.

PSATHAS, G. (ed.) (1973) Phenomenological Sociology. New York: John Wiley.

RABINOW, P. (1977) Reflections on Fieldwork in Morocco. Berkeley: Univ. of California Press.

RABINOW, P. and W. M. SULLIVAN (eds.) (1979) Interpretive Social Science. Berkeley: Univ. of California Press.

RATCLIFFE, J. W. (1983) "Notions of validity in qualitative research methodology." Knowledge: Creation, Diffusion, Utilization 5 (2): 147-167.

REASONS, P. and J. ROWAN (1981) "Issues of validity in new paradigm research," pp. 239-250 in P. Reasons and J. Rowan (eds.) Human Inquiry: A Sourcebook of New Paradigm Research. Chichester: John Wiley.

RENNIE, D. L., J. R. PHILLIPS, and G. K. QUARTARO (in press) "Grounded theory: a promising approach to conceptualization in psychology?" Canadian Psychology 29.

REEVES SANDAY, P. (1979) "The ethnographic paradigm(s)." Qualitative Methodology 24 (December): 527-538.

REINHARZ, S. (1979) On Becoming a Social Scientist: From Survey Research and Participant Observation to Experiential Analysis. San Francisco: Jossey-Bass.

RICHARDS, L. and T. RICHARDS (1987) "Qualitative data analysis: can computers do it?" Australian and New Zealand J. of Sociology 23 (1): 23-35.

RIST, R. (1977) "On the relations among educational research paradigms: from disdain to detente." Anthropology and Education 8: 42-49.

ROGERS, C. R. (1945) "The non-directive method as a technique for social research." Amer. J. of Sociology 50 (4): 279-283.

SACKS, H., E. A. SCHEGLOFF, and G. JEFFERSON (1974) "A simplest systematics for the organization of turn-taking for conversation." Language 50: 696-735.

SALAMONE, F. (1977) "The methodological significance of the lying informant." Anthropology Q. 50: 117-124.

SAMPSON, R. (1972a) "Qualitative research and motivation research," pp. 7-27 in R. M. Worcester (ed.) Consumer Market Research Handbook. London: McGraw-Hill.

SAMPSON, R. (1972b) "Using the repertory grid test." J. of Marketing Research 9 (February): 78-81.

SCHATZMAN, L. and A. STRAUSS (1973) Field Research: Strategies for a Natural Sociology. Englewood Cliffs, NJ: Prentice-Hall.

SCHEGLOFF, E. and H. SACKS (1973) "Opening up closings." Semiotica (8): 289-327.

SCHIFFRIN, D. (1977) "Opening encounters." Amer. Soc. Rev. 42 (5): 679-691.

SCHWARTZ, G. and P. BECKER (1971) "Participant observation and the discovery of meaning." Philosophy of the Social Sciences 1: 279-298.

SCHWARTZ, H. and J. JACOBS (1979) Qualitative Sociology. New York: Free Press.

SCHWARTZ, M. S. and C. G. SCHWARTZ (1955) "Problems in participant observation." Amer. J. of Sociology 60 (4): 343-353.

SEELEY, J. R., R. A. SIM, and E. W. LOOSELY (1956) Crestwood Heights: A Study of the Culture of Suburban Life. Toronto: Univ. of Toronto Press.

SHAFFIR, W. B., R. A. STEBBINS, and A. TUROWETZ (eds.) (1980) Fieldwork Experience: Qualitative Approaches to Social Research. New York: St. Martin's.

SHERRY, J. F., Jr. (1987) "Keeping the monkeys away from the typewriters: an anthropologist's view of the consumer behavior odyssey," pp. 370-373 in

M. Wallendorf and P. Anderson (eds.) Advances in Consumer Research. Provo, UT: Association for Consumer Research.

SIEBER, S. D. (1973) "The integration of fieldwork and survey methods." Amer. J. of Sociology 78: 1335-1359.

SILVERMAN, D. (1985) Qualitative Methodology and Sociology. Aldershot, Hampshire: Gower.

SMITH, J. K. and L. HESHUSIUS (1986) "Closing down the conversation: the end of the quantitative-qualitative debate among educational inquirers." Educ. Researcher 19: 4-12.

SNELL, D. A. (1987) "Focus groups: theory and analysis." Canadian J. of Marketing Research 6: 2-9.

SPRADLEY, J. P. (1979) The Ethnographic Interview. New York: Holt, Reinhardt & Winston.

SPROULL, L. S. and R. F. SPROULL (1982) "Managing and analyzing behavioral records: explorations in nonnumeric data analysis." Human Organization 41 (4): 283-290.

SRINIVAS, M. N. et al. (eds.) (1979) The Fieldwork and the Field. Delhi: Oxford Univ. Press.

STAKE, R. E. (1978) "The case study method in social inquiry." Educ. Researcher 7 (2): 5-8.

STEBBINS, R. A. (1972) " The unstructured research interview as incipient interpersonal relationship." Sociology and Social Research 56 (2): 164-177.

STOCKING, G. W., Jr.(1983) "The ethnographer's magic: fieldwork in British anthropology from Tylor to Malinowski," pp 70-120 in G. W. Stocking, Jr. (ed.) Observers Observed: Essays on Ethnographic Fieldwork. Madison: Univ. of Wisconsin Press.

STRAUSS, A. and L. SCHATZMAN (1955) "Cross-class interviewing: an analysis of interaction and communication styles." Human Organization 14 (2): 28-31.

SULLIVAN, H. S. (1954) The Psychiatric Interview. New York: Norton.

TAGG, S. K. (1985) "Life story interview and their interpretation," pp. 163-199 in M. Brenner, J. Brown, and D. Canter (eds.) The Research Interview: Uses and Approaches. London: Academic Press.

THOMAS, J. (ed.) (1983) "The Chicago School." Urban Life 11 (4) (Special issue): 908-944.

TREND, M. G. (1979) "On the reconciliation of qualitative and quantitative analyses: a case study," pp. 68-86 in T. D. Cook and C. S. Reichardt (eds.) Qualitative and Quantitative methods in Evaluation Research. Beverly Hills, CA: Sage.

TROW, M. (1957) "Comment on participant observation and interviewing: a comparison." Human Organization 16 (3): 33-35.

TRUZZI, M. (ed.) (1974) Verstehen: Subjective Understanding in the Social Sciences. Reading, MA: Addison-Wesley.

TURNER, V. (1967) "Muchona the Hornet, interpreter of religion," pp. 131-150 in V. Turner (ed.) The Forest of Symbols. Ithaca: Cornell Univ. Press.

VAN MAANEN, J. (ed.) (1982) Varieties of Qualitative Research. Beverly Hills, CA: Sage.

VAN MAANEN, J. (ed.) (1983) Qualitative Methodology. Beverly Hills, CA: Sage.

VAN MAANEN, J. (1988) Tales of the Field: On Writing Ethnography. Chicago: Univ. of Chicago Press.

VAN MAANEN, J. , J. M. DABBS, and R. R. FAULKNER (1982) Varieties of Qualitative Research. Beverly Hills, CA: Sage.
VAN VELSEN, J. (1967) "The extended-case method and situational analysis," pp. in A. L. Epstein (ed.) The Craft of Anthropology. London: Social Science Paperbacks.
VIDICH, A. J. (1955) "Participant observation and the collection and interpretation of data." Amer. J. of Sociology 60 (4): 354-360.
VIDICH, A. J. and G. SHAPIRO (1955) "A comparison of participant observation and survey data." Amer. Soc. Rev. 20: 28-33.
VOGT, E. Z. (1956) "Interviewing water-dowers." Amer. J. of Sociology 62 (2): 198.
VON HOFFMAN, N. and S. W. CASSIDY (1956) "Interviewing Negro Pentecostals." Amer. J. of Sociology 62 (2): 195-197.
WALLENDORF, M. (1987) "On the road again: the nature of qualitative research on the consumer behavior odyssey," pp. 374-375 in M. Wallendorf and P. Anderson (eds.) Advances in Consumer Research. Provo, UT: Assn. for Consumer Research.
WARNER, L. and P. S. LUNT (1941) The Social Life of a Modern Community. New Haven, CT: Yale Univ. Press.
WATSON, L. C. and M. B. WATSON-FRANKE (1985) Interpreting Life History: An Anthropological Inquiry. New Brunswick: Rutgers Univ. Press.
WAX, M. and L. J. SHAPIRO (1956) "Repeated interviewing." Amer. J. of Sociology 62 (2): 215-217.
WAX, R. H. (1952) "Reciprocity as a field technique." Human Organization 11 (3): 34-37.
WELLS, W. (1986) "Truth and consequences." J. of Advertising Research 26 (3): RC 13-16.
WERNER, O. and G. M. SCHOEPFLE (1987) Systematic Fieldwork: Foundations of Ethnography and Interviewing. Beverly Hills, CA: Sage.
WHITTAKER, E. (1981) "Anthropological ethics, fieldwork and epistemological disjunctures." Philosophy of the Social Sciences 11: 437-451.
WHITTAKER, E. (1985) The Mainland Haole: White Experience in Hawaii. New York: Columbia Univ. Press.
WHYTE, W. F. (1955) Street Corner Society (enlarged ed.). Chicago: Univ. of Chicago Press.
WHYTE, W. F. (1957) "On asking indirect questions." Human Organization 15 (4): 21-25.
WHYTE, W. F. (1960) "Interviewing in field research," pp. 352-374 in R. N. Adams and J. J. Preiss (eds.) Human Organization Research. Homewood, IL: Dorsey.
WHYTE, W. F. (1984) Learning from the Field: A Guide from Experience. Beverly Hills, CA: Sage.
WILLEMS, E. P. and H. L. RAUSCH (eds.) (1969) Naturalistic Viewpoints in Psychological Research. New York: Holt.
WILLIAMS, J. A., Jr. (1964) "Interviewer-respondent interaction: a study of bias in the information interview." Sociometry 27 (3): 338-352.
WILSON, S. (1977) "The use of ethnographic techniques in educational research." Rev. of Educational Research 47 (2): 245-265.
ZIMMERMAN, D. H. and D. L. WIEDER (1977) "The diary: diary interview method." Urban Life 5 (4): 479-498.

ABOUT THE AUTHOR

GRANT McCRACKEN is Associate Professor in the Department of Consumer Studies at the University of Guelph, Guelph, Ontario, Canada. He received his Ph.D. in anthropology from the University of Chicago in 1981. He has been a Visiting Scholar in the Department of Social Anthropology at the University of Cambridge and a Killam Postdoctoral Fellow at the Department of Anthropology and Sociology at the University of British Columbia. He is the author of some 20 articles and a book, *Culture and Consumption: New Approaches to the Symbolic Character of Consumer Goods and Activities* (Bloomington: University of Indiana Press, 1988).